KW-222-220

EFFECTIVE ENTERPRISE AND CHANGE MANAGEMENT

ALAN H. ANDERSON
and
DENNIS BARKER

658 406
AND

Copyright © Alan H. Anderson and Dennis Barker 1996

The right of Alan H. Anderson and Dennis Barker to be identified as authors of this work has been asserted in accordance with the Copyright, Designs and Patents Act 1988.

First published 1996

First published in USA
2 4 6 8 10 9 7 5 3 1

Blackwell Publishers Ltd
108 Cowley Road
Oxford OX4 1JF
UK

Blackwell Publishers Inc.
238 Main Street
Cambridge, Massachusetts 02142
USA

All rights reserved. Except for the quotation of short passages for the purposes of criticism and review, no part of this publication may be reproduced, stored in a retrieval system, or transmitted, in any form or by any means, electronic, mechanical, photocopying, recording or otherwise, without the prior permission of the publisher.

Except in the United States of America, this book is sold subject to the condition that it shall not, by way of trade or otherwise, be lent, resold, hired out, or otherwise circulated without the publisher's prior consent in any form of binding or cover other than that in which it is published and without a similar condition including this condition being imposed on the subsequent purchaser.

British Library Cataloguing in Publication Data

A CIP catalogue record for this book is available from the British Library.

Library of Congress Cataloging-in-Publication Data

Anderson, Alan H., 1950–
    Effective enterprise and change management / Alan H. Anderson and Dennis Barker.
       p. cm. – (Effective management)
    Includes bibliographical references and index.
    ISBN 0-631-19124-0 (pbk.: alk. paper)
      1. Organizational change—Management.
    I. Barker, Dennis. II. Title. III. Series.
    HD58.8.A68 1995   95-14747
    658.4'06 – dc20   CIP

ISBN 0-631-19124-0

Designed and typeset in Plantin by VAP Group Ltd., Kidlington, Oxfordshire

Printed in Great Britain by T.J. Press, Padstow,Cornwall.

This book is printed on acid-free paper

EFFECTIVE

ENTERPRISE AND

CHANGE

MANAGEMENT

WITHDRAWN
FROM THE LIBRARY OF
UNIVERSITY OF ULSTER

EFFECTIVE MANAGEMENT

100368921

Effective Management
Series Editor: Alan H. Anderson

Effective Personnel Management
Alan H. Anderson

Effective Business Policy
Alan H. Anderson and Dennis Barker

Effective General Management
Alan H. Anderson

Effective Organizational Behaviour
Alan H. Anderson and Anna Kyprianou

Effective Labour Relations
Alan H. Anderson

Effective Marketing
Alan H. Anderson and Thelma Dobson

Effective International Marketing
Alan H. Anderson, Thelma Dobson and James Patterson

Effective Marketing Communications
Alan H. Anderson and David Kleiner

Effective Entrepreneurship
Alan H. Anderson and Peter Woodcock

Effective Enterprise and Change Management
Alan H. Anderson and Dennis Barker

Effective Accounting Management
Alan H. Anderson and Eileen Nix

Effective Financial Management
Alan H. Anderson and Richard Ciechan

Effective Operations Management
Alan H. Anderson and Simon Speller

Effective Market Research
Alan H. Anderson and Bal Charnsartar

Effective Information Management
Alan H. Anderson and Margaret Thompson

Effective Self-Development
Alan H. Anderson, Dennis Barker and Peter Critten

Contents

Figures

Boxes

Activities

Introduction to the Series

❝ He that has done nothing has known nothing. ❞

Carlyle

The Concept

In this series 'effective' means getting results. By taking an action approach to management, or the stewardship of an organization, the whole series allows people to create and develop their skills of effectiveness. This interrelated series gives the underpinning knowledge base and the application of functional and generic skills of the effective manager who gets results.

Key qualities of the effective manager include:

- **functional expertise** in the various disciplines of management;
- an understanding of the **organizational context**;
- an appreciation of the **external environment**;
- **self-awareness** and the power of **self-development**.

These qualities must fuse in a climate of **enterprise**.

Management is results-oriented so action is at a premium. The basis of this activity is **skills** underpinned by our qualities. In turn these skills can be based on a discipline or a function, and be universal or generic.

The Approach of the Series

These key qualities of effective management are the core of the current sixteen books of the series. The areas covered by the series at present are:

People management	*Effective Personnel Management*
	Effective Labour Relations
	Effective Organizational Behaviour
	Effective Self-Development
Finance	*Effective Financial Management*
	Effective Accounting Management
	Effective Information Management
Marketing and sales	*Effective Marketing*
	Effective International Marketing
	Effective Marketing Communications
	Effective Market Research

xiii

Enterprise management   *Effective General Management*
Effective Business Policy
Effective Enterprise and Change Management
Effective Entrepreneurship
Effective Operations Management: a quality perspective

The key attributes of the effective manager are all dealt with in the series, and we will pinpoint where they are emphasized:

- *Functional expertise.* The four main disciplines of management – finance, marketing, enterprise/operations and personnel management – make up sixteen books. These meet the needs of specialist disciplines and allow a wider appreciation of other functions.

- *Organizational context.* All the 'people' books – the specialist one on *Effective Organizational Behaviour*, and also *Effective Personnel Management* and *Effective Labour Relations* – cover this area. The resourcing/control issues are met in the 'finance' texts, *Effective Financial Management*, *Effective Information Management* and *Effective Accounting Management*. Every case activity is given some organizational context.

- *External environment.* One book, *Effective Business Policy*, is dedicated to this subject. Environmental contexts apply in every book of the series: especially in *Effective Entrepreneurship*, *Effective General Management*, and in all of the 'marketing' texts – *Effective Marketing*, *Effective International Marketing*, *Effective Marketing Communications* and *Effective Market Research*.

- *Self-awareness/self-development.* To a great extent management development is manager development, so we have one generic skill (see later) devoted to this topic running through each book. The subject is examined in detail in *Effective General Management*, and *Effective Self-Development* is devoted to the topic.

- *Enterprise.* The *Effective Entrepreneurship* text is allied to *Effective Enterprise and Change Management* to give insights into this whole area through all the developing phases of the firm. The marketing and policy books also revolve around this theme. Quality is 'operationalized' in *Effective Operations Management* to stimulate enterprise across all organizations.

Skills

The functional skills are inherent within the discipline-based texts. In addition, running through the series are the following generic skills:
- self-development
- teamwork
- communications
- numeracy/IT
- decisions

These generic skills are universal managerial skills which occur to some degree in every manager's job.

Format/Structure of Each Book

Each book is subdivided into six units. These are self-contained, in order to facilitate learning, but interrelated, in order to give an effective holistic view. Each book also has an introduction with an outline of the book's particular theme.

Each unit has *learning objectives* with an overview/summary of the unit.

Boxes appear in every unit of every book. They allow a different perspective from the main narrative and analysis. Research points, examples, controversy and theory are all expanded upon in these boxes. They are numbered by unit in each book, e.g. 'Box PM1.1' for the first box in Unit One of *Effective Personnel Management.*

Activities, numbered in the same way, permeate the series. These action-oriented forms of learning cover cases, questionnaires, survey results, financial data, market research information, etc. The skills which can be assessed in each one are noted in the code at the top right of the activity by having the square next to them ticked. That is, if we are assuming numeracy then the square beside Numeracy is ticked (✓), and so on. The weighting given to these skills will depend on the activity, the tutors'/learners' needs, and the overall weighting of the skills as noted in the section below on 'The Series: Learning, Activities, Skills and Compatibility', with problem solving dominating in most cases.

Common cases run through the series. Functional approaches are added to these core cases to show the same organization from different perspectives. This simulates the complexity of reality.

Instructor's manual

For each book in the series, there is an *instructor's manual*. This is not quite the 'answers' to the activities, but it does contain some indicative ideas for them (coded accordingly), which will help to stimulate discussion and thought.

The Audience

The series is for all those who wish to be effective managers. As such, it is a series for management development on an international scale, and embraces both management education and management training. In management education, the emphasis still tends to be on cognitive or knowledge inputs; in management training, it still tends to be on skills and techniques. We need both theory and practice, with the facility to try out these functions and skills through a range of scenarios in a 'safe' learning environment. This series is unique in encompassing these perspectives and bridging the gulf between the academic and vocational sides of business management.

Academically the series is pitched at the DMS/DBA types of qualification, which lead on to an MA/MBA after the second year. Undergraduates following business degrees or management studies will benefit from the series in their final years. Distance learners will also find the series useful, as will those studying managerial subjects for professional examinations. The competency approach and the movement towards Accredited Prior Learning and National Vocational Qualifications are underpinned by the knowledge inputs, while the activities will provide useful simulations for these approaches to management learning.

This developmental series gives an opportunity for self-improvement. Individuals may wish to enhance their managerial potential by developing themselves without institutional backing by working through the whole series. It can also be used to underpin corporate training programmes, and acts as a useful design vehicle for specialist inputs from organizations. We are happy to pursue these various options with institutions or corporations.

The approach throughout the series combines skills, knowledge and application to create and develop the effective manager. Any comments or thoughts from participants in this interactive process will be welcomed.

Alan H. Anderson
Melbourn, Cambridge

The Series: Learning, Activities, Skills and Compatibility

The emphasis on skills and activities as vehicles of learning makes this series unique. Behavioural change, or learning, is developed through a two-pronged approach.

First, there is the **knowledge-based (cognitive)** approach to learning. This is found in the main text and in the boxes. These cognitive inputs form the traditional method of learning based on the principle of receiving and understanding information. In this series, there are four main knowledge inputs covering the four main managerial functions: marketing/sales, operations/enterprise, people, and accounting/finance. In addition, these disciplines are augmented by a strategic overview covering policy making and general management. An example of this first approach may be illustrative. In the case of marketing, the learner is confronted with a model of the internal and external environments. Thereafter the learner must digest, reflect, and understand the importance of this model to the whole of the subject.

Second, there is the **activity-based** approach to learning, which emphasizes the application of knowledge and skill through techniques. This approach is vital in developing effectiveness. It is seen from two levels of learning:

1 The use and application of *specific skills*. This is the utilization of your cognitive knowledge in a practical manner. These skills emanate from the cognitive aspect of learning, so they are functional skills, specific to the discipline.

   For example, the learner needs to understand the concept of job analysis before he or she tackles an activity that requires the drawing up of a specific job evaluation programme. So knowledge is not seen for its own sake, but is applied and becomes a specific functional skill.

2 The use and application of *generic skills*. These are universal skills which every manager uses irrespective of the wider external environment, the organization, the function and the job. This is seen, for example, in the ability to make clear decisions on the merits of a case. This skill of decision making is found in most of the activities.

There is a relationship between the specific functional skills and the generic skills. The specific functional skills stand alone, but the generic skills cut across them. See figure SK.1.

In this series we use activities to cover both the specific functional and the generic skills. There are five generic skills. We shall examine each of them in turn.

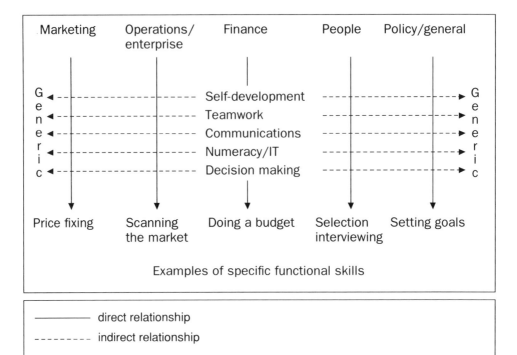

Figure SK.1 Series skills matrix: functional and generic skills.

Self-Development

The learner must take responsibility for his or her learning as well as 'learning how to learn'. Time management, work scheduling and organizing the work are involved in the procedural sense. From a learning perspective, sound aspects of learning, from motivation to reward, need to be clarified and understood. The physical process of learning, including changing knowledge, skills and attitudes, may be involved. Individual goals and aspirations need to be recognized alongside the task goals. The ultimate aim of this skill is to facilitate learning transfer to new situations and environments.

Examples of this skill include:

- establishing and clarifying work goals;
- developing procedures and methods of work;
- building key learning characteristics into the process;
- using procedural learning;
- applying insightful learning;
- creating personal developmental plans;
- integrating these personal developmental plans with work goals.

Teamwork

Much of our working lives is concerned with groups. Effective teamwork is thus at a premium. This involves meeting both the task objectives and the socio-emotional processes within the group. This skill can be used for groups in a training or educational context. It can be a bridge between decision making and an awareness of self-development.

Examples of this skill include:

- clarifying the task need of the group;
- receiving, collating, ordering and rendering information;
- discussing, chairing and teamwork within the group;
- identifying the socio-emotional needs and group processes;
- linking these needs and processes to the task goals of the group.

Communications

This covers information and attitude processing within and between individuals. Oral and written communications are important because of the gamut of 'information and attitudinal' processing within the individual. At one level communication may mean writing a report, at another it could involve complex interpersonal relationships.

Examples of this skill include:

- understanding the media, aids, the message and methods;
- overcoming blockages;
- listening;
- presenting a case or commenting on the views of others;
- writing;
- designing material and systems for others to understand your communications.

Numeracy/IT

Managers need a core mastery of numbers and their application. This mastery is critical for planning, control, co-ordination, organization and, above all else, decision making. Numeracy/IT are not seen as skills for their own sake. Here, they are regarded as the means to an end. These skills enable information and data to be utilized by the effective manager. In particular these skills are seen as an adjunct to decision making.

Examples of this skill include:

- gathering information;
- processing and testing information;

- using measures of accuracy, reliability, probability etc.;
- applying appropriate software packages;
- extrapolating information and trends for problem solving.

Decision Making

Management is very much concerned with solving problems and making decisions. As group decisions are covered under teamwork, the emphasis in this decision-making skill is placed on the individual.

Decision making can involve a structured approach to problem solving with appropriate aims and methods. Apart from the 'scientific' approach, we can employ also an imaginative vision towards decision making. One is rational, the other is more like brainstorming.

Examples of this skill include:

- setting objectives and establishing criteria;
- seeking, gathering and processing information;
- deriving alternatives;
- using creative decision making;
- action planning and implementation.

This is *the* skill of management and is given primary importance in the generic skills within the activities as a reflection of everyday reality.

Before we go about learning how to develop into effective managers, it is important to understand the general principles of learning. Both the knowledge-based and the activity-based approaches are set within the environment of these principles. The series has been written to relate to Anderson's sound principles of learning which were developed in *Successful Training Practice*.

- *Motivation* – intrinsic motivation is stimulated by the range and depth of the subject matter and assisted by an action orientation.
- *Knowledge of results* – ongoing feedback is given through the instructor's manual for each book in the series.
- *Scale learning* – each text is divided into six units, which facilitates part learning.
- *Self-pacing* – a map of the unit with objectives, content and an overview helps learners to pace their own progress.
- *Transfer* – realism is enhanced through lifelike simulations which assist learning transfer.
- *Discovery learning* – the series is geared to the learner using self-insight to stimulate learning.
- *Self-development* – self-improvement and an awareness of how we go about learning underpin the series.

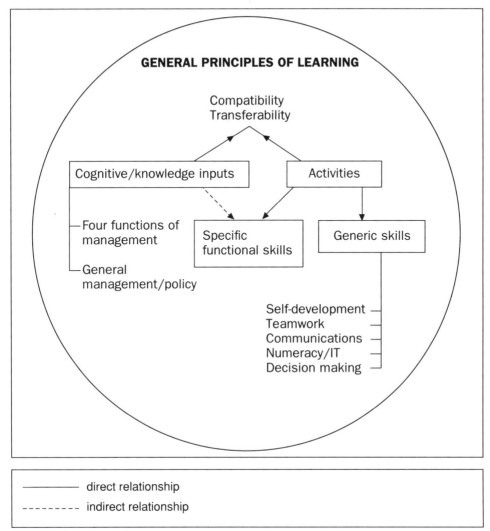

Figure SK.2 Series learning strategy.

- *Active learning* – every activity is based upon this critical component of successful learning.

From what has been said so far, the learning strategy of the series can be outlined in diagrammatic form. (See figure SK.2.)

In figure SK.2, 'compatibility and transferability' are prominent because the learning approach of the series is extremely compatible with the learning approaches of current initiatives in management development. This series is related to a range of learning classification being used in education and training. Consequently it meets the needs of other leading training systems and learning taxonomies. See figures SK.3–SK.6.

Functional knowledge and skills	An educational classification
People:	
Personnel management	—— People
Labour relations	
Organizational behaviour	
Self-development	
Marketing/sales:	
Marketing	—— Marketing
Marketing communications	
International marketing	
Market research	
Operations/enterprise:	
Entrepreneurship	—— Operations/enterprise
Enterprise and change	
Quality and operations	
Finance:	
Accounting management	—— Finance
Finance	
Information management	
Policy/management:	
Policy	—— Business environment/
General management	business administration

Generic skills

Self-development	—— Managing and developing self
Teamwork	—— Working with and relating to others
Communications	Communications
	Applying design and creativity
Decisions	Managing tasks and solving problems
Numeracy/IT	Applying technology
	Applying numeracy

—————— direct relationship

- - - - - - - indirect relationship

Figure SK.3 Series knowledge and skills related to an educational classification.

Source: Adapted from Business Technician and Education Council, 'Common skills and experience of BTEC programmes'.

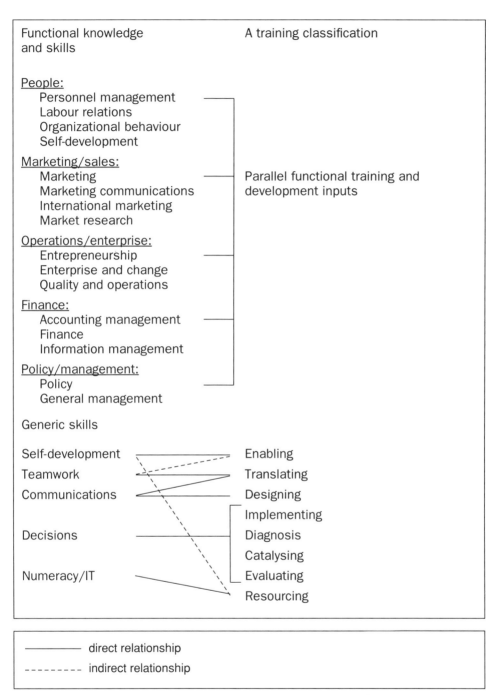

Figure SK.4 Series knowledge and skills related to a training classification.

Source: Adapted from J.A.G. Jones, 'Training intervention strategies', ITS Monograph no. 2 (Industrial Training Services Ltd, London, 1983), and experience of development programmes.

Functional knowledge and skills	MCI competency
People:	Managing people
Personnel management	
Labour relations	
Organizational behaviour	
Self-development	
Marketing/sales:	
Marketing	Managing operations and
Marketing communications	managing information
International marketing	(plus new texts pending)
Market research	
Operations/enterprise:	
Entrepreneurship	
Enterprise and change	
Quality and operations	
Finance:	Managing finance
Accounting management	
Finance	
Information management	
Policy/management:	Managing context
Policy	
General management	
Generic skills	
Self-development	Managing oneself
Teamwork	Managing others
Communications	Using intellect
Decisions	Planning
Numeracy/IT	

———— direct relationship

- - - - - - - indirect relationship

Figure SK.5 Series knowledge and skills related to Management Charter Initiative (MCI) competencies.

Source: Adapted from MCI, *Diploma Level Guidelines* (MCI, London, n.d.).

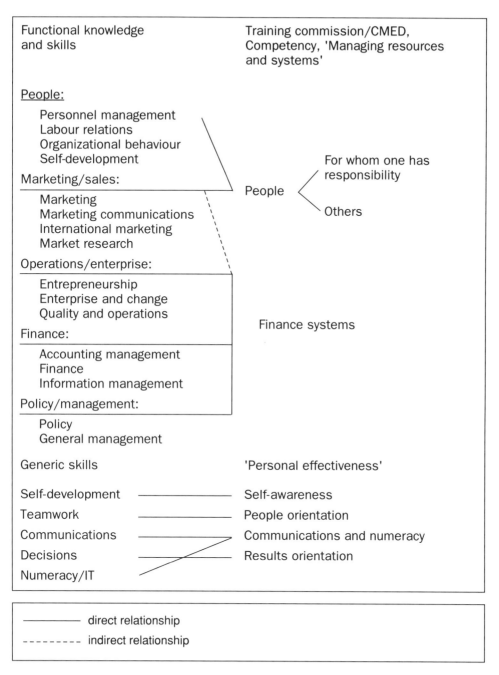

Figure SK.6   Series knowledge and skills related to Training Commission/Council for Management Education (CMED) competencies.

Source: Adapted from Training Commission/CMED, 'Classifying the components of management competencies' (Training Commission, London, 1988).

Preface

> 66 We are all born with enterprise. None of us would survive with-
> out enterprise. Every baby and toddler demonstrates every day
> . . . that early in life we all have an abundance of enterprise,
> initiative, the ability to spot an opportunity and take rapid
> advantage of it. 99
>
> *Cited by Seldon*[1]

Outline Themes

Enterprise and entrepreneurship

The spirit of enterprise runs through the *Effective Entrepreneurship* book of this series.[2] To foment growth, if not survival itself, this enterprise, harnessing the business to marketing opportunity, must continue through the entrepreneurial phase to the more managerial phases of an organization. Success will depend on this marketing opportunism – tempered by ethical considerations.

Once we move away from the owner-entrepreneur concept, enterprise problems start to appear in medium-sized managed organizations. Managing such enterprise is the subject of this book. The entrepreneurial phase becomes overtaken by managerial evolution, which in turn lays the foundations for structured bureaucracy, with its closely delineated functions or disciplines of management, whereby specialists have a vision of their particular expertise and are often blinkered to the overall need for enterprise in the organization. Managers and staff become trapped within their functional disciplines.[3] Some attempts to escape this functional strait-jacket include project teams, matrix structures[4] and, the latest fad, process re-engineering. (See Boxes ECM5.5 and ECM5.6.)

The concept of entrepreneurship has been grafted on to some larger organizations through intrapreneurship as well. However, we cannot really escape the point that by definition there is a split between the entrepreneur-owner and management,[5] and at best intrapreneurship is a mixed solution. Others have argued that the entrepreneur role is a fundamental cluster of all managers' jobs which in turn forms an integrated *Gestalt* of roles.[6] Perhaps this is more of an aspiration than a reality, other than in, say, the marketing and corporate or strategic policy areas.

The spirit of the entrepreneur

If a gulf lies between entrepreneur and manager, a chasm exists in many medium-sized organizations between entrepreneur and worker. The entrepreneur can be seen as 'one who undertakes an enterprise'.[7] This implies ownership or at least some stake in the whole organization. It is felt that the pure entrepreneurial spirit is not transferable to non-owners of the organization.

The undertaking of innovation is down to a very select group of people at the top who have a definite stake (greater than most), while the rest of the workforce has little real ownership of the firm. Hence this spirit of entrepreneurship may be difficult to replicate in larger organizations under the control of managers.

Now some attempts at widening the ownership base are being made. Elsewhere in the series there is a review of the participative and involvement schemes of management,[8] which puts forward the view that many of these schemes give some involvement in issues concerning terms and conditions of employment, a limited share in managerial decision making, little or no representation at government/policy-making level, and, apart from modest share option schemes or some more obscure co-operative schemes, little participation in ownership.[9] Other attempts at 'ownership' include the personalized approach of 'empowerment', with individuals taking more control of their working lives, linked to some participative/consultative style of management. Style, however, is not substance. Empowerment may give greater self-awareness and self-satisfaction but ultimately it does not impact on the economic ownership of the organization.

So entrepreneurship may be difficult to replicate in medium-sized and larger organizations – particularly where the founding entrepreneur has moved on and/or management has been installed. Can we have a spirit of enterprise, then, which is lower down the scale than pure entrepreneurship?

We believe so.

A culture of enterprise and change

Fundamental to our views is the ability of an organization to adapt and to adopt. Change management and enterprise must fuse. Management needs to adopt a vision of innovation, adventure and opportunism tempered by ethical considerations. The organization and its workers must become market-oriented, so that the concern for quality is dominant in order to meet customer needs. The business and its environments must be known and appreciated by all employees. Rewards for effort, merit and ability should not be the monopoly of senior managers, and ownership of the organization should genuinely be spread throughout the organization to real stakeholders who have an interest in the business.

We need a culture of enterprise. This culture will allow the organization to move from 'steady state' or relative decline through to forced growth by being able to exploit opportunity and reduce threats in the external environments.

Enterprise management, like entrepreneurship, must involve an ethical dimension, and we argue this case in the 'enterpreneurship' book.[10] A culture of enterprise is not an encouragement to the barrow-boy, 'get-rich-quick' mentality which pervaded parts of the UK in the mid- to late-1980s.

Entrepreneurship is not just opportunism, and neither is enterprise management. Entrepreneurship is a type of informal business policy, a marrying up of individual strengths and environmental opportunity. Policy in larger firms can become ossified through bureaucratic machinery and processes.[11] Here we need to be able to match organizational (not individual) strengths to environmental opportunities as well as minimizing organizational weakness and countering environmental threats. A philosophy of enterprise with its associated culture should facilitate these more formalized policies – without losing the spirit of adventure, innovation and marketing orientation.

To summarize, enterprise and change permeate this book as the means of adoption of and adaptation to environmental and organizational influences. We are not suggesting some type of Stalinist permanent disruption or some Maoist permanent revolution, as change should be managed for the sake of enterprise and not become worshipped for its own sake.

The Learning Objectives

The learning objectives of this book are:
- To examine the concept and application of change.
- To examine the concept and application of enterprise.
- To fuse change and enterprise as our two perspectives.
- To conduct an external scan of environments from our two perspectives.
- To conduct an internal scan of organizations from our two perspectives.
- To trace the development of change and the organization through 'steady state', 'decline' and 'growth'.
- To put forward appropriate policies of enterprise in these phases of change.

Overview of the Format and Content

As the format of the generic skills and the activities has been covered in the series introduction, the content will be emphasized here. There is a main narrative-cum-analysis which excludes the boxes. (The function of the boxes is explained in the series introduction.)

The content aims to be international in its appeal and also to embrace various sectors of management, from commercial to public sector or voluntarist organizations, where the commonweal or service must be reconciled with the need for enterprise in our economy. The work is geared more towards medium-sized or larger organizations.

So enterprise, the ability to grasp the external opportunity and mobilize internal resources, must be placed in the dynamic milieu of the external environment, which is always changing. The central plank is change. We analyse the concept, its dynamics, its techniques and associated problems in the first unit.

Change on its own terms is not enough, as it can emanate from and influence the wider external environments and the internal organization. So in Unit 2 (the external environment) and in Unit 3 (the business environment of the organization), we analyse these variables of change and enterprise.

Next we formulate an ideal type based on a relatively 'steady state' between the organization and its environments (Unit 4). The Seven S technique[12] and the TPF approach[13] are used in this analysis.

We then alter the equilibrium by looking at negative change or decline in Unit 5 and positive, growth-related change in Unit 6. Triggers of change, approaches and coping or enhancing strategies are pursued.

We do not put forward some linear progression from a steady state through growth to decline. We could have used a product-life-cycle approach to the organization to show an ageing process or an evolutionary–revolutionary synthesis, as used by the likes of Greiner.[14] Some organizations can stay in these phases for ever and a day, depending on the enterprise–change conditions, while others can move to and fro over the three 'states' outlined in Units 4, 5 and 6. On the other hand, we have idealized the states, for there can also be some hangover from each phase into the next stage.

In summary, to understand enterprise we must understand change, and change without enterprise is a self-defeating and expensive policy to pursue.

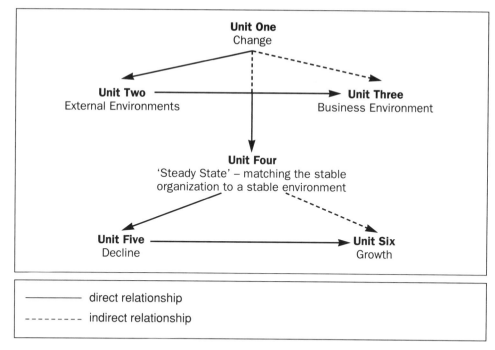

Figure ECM0.1   Interaction between the units in this book.

Notes

1   Seldon, R., 'The rhetoric of enterprise', in *Enterprise Culture*, eds R. Kent and N. Abercrombie (Routledge, London, 1991).

2   Anderson, A.H. and Woodcock, P., *Effective Entrepreneurship* (Blackwell Publishers, Oxford, forthcoming).

3   This functionalist strait-jacket is developed as one of the main premises of Anderson, A.H., *Effective General Management* (Blackwell Publishers, Oxford, forthcoming).

4   There seems to be a host of structural experiments intended to loosen the reins of bureaucracy and to set up a freer, more 'organic' type of organization. See Williams, A., who examines both structural and process 'interventions' in 'Organisational development', in *Managing Human Resources*, eds A.G. Cowling and C.J.B. Mailer (Arnold, London, 1990).

5   See Burnham's classic thesis in Burnham, J., *The Managerial Revolution: what is happening in the world* (John Day, New York, 1941).

6   Mintzberg, H., *The Nature of Managerial Work* (Harper and Row, New York, 1973).

7   *Chambers Twentieth Century Dictionary*, ed. W. Geddes (Chambers, Edinburgh, 1956).

8   See Anderson, A.H., *Effective Labour Relations* (Blackwell Publishers, Oxford, 1994).

9   See Walker, K.F., 'Workers participation in management: concepts and reality', in *Industrial Relations and the Wider Society*, eds B. Barnett, E. Rhodes and J. Beishen (Open University Press, Milton Keynes, 1975).

10 Anderson and Woodcock, *Effective Entrepreneurship*.

11 We note this potential for ossification in Anderson, A.H., and Barker, D., *Effective Business Policy* (Blackwell Publishers, Oxford, 1994), which continues with some of the issues raised in this text – although it is geared to a larger organization and the issues confronting that type of business.

12 Waterman, R.H., Peters, T.J. and Phillips, J.R., 'Structure is not organisation', *Business Horizons*, June (1980). See also Waterman, R.H., 'The seven elements of strategic fit', *Journal of Business Strategy* (1982).

13 Anderson, *Effective General Management*.

14 Greiner, L.E., 'Evolution and revolution as organisations grow', *Harvard Business Review*, July/August (1972).

ECM Unit One

Change

Learning Objectives

After completing this unit you should be able to:
- explain the nature of change in organizations;
- explain why organizations should change;
- explain and identify resistance to change;
- explain how managers can adapt to change;
- understand the best ways to make decisions;
- introduce change into your organization successfully;
- apply the generic skills.

Contents

ECM Unit One

❝ Change management programmes can be a significant burden on senior management, tying up considerable time in programme management . . . A major task is to ensure that the change machine does not get out of control. ❞

M. Jeans, a partner with the consultancy firm KPMG [1]

A. Overview

Change is seen as being all-pervasive across organizations, yet organizational stability and the natural conservatism of many managers can inhibit its diffusion. We advocate a planned approach to change management, while accepting that day-to-day exigencies may mean considerable improvization and departure from plans. So piecemeal planning is integral to flexibility in management, but long-term planning can ensure the survival and growth of the organization – assuming that it is linked to enterprise.

We envisage organizations interacting with their external environments and passing through various stages of a 'steady state', decline/recovery or growth. Change and enterprise interact.

The resistance to change is examined in detail, as this can frustrate if not destroy the whole process of change management.

This unit is consolidated by examining techniques of how to manage change successfully.

B. Introduction to Change

In this unit we examine change and the way it impinges on your organization with a view to enabling you to manage change effectively. We will explain various ways of recognizing the need for change and identifying the different types of resistance change will meet. Ways of managing change will then be explained and the ways decisions have to be made to take action explored.

In the book *Effective Business Policy* in this series we have avoided the use of the term 'strategy'. We believe that strategies, other than the generic strategies of cost leadership, differentiation and focus, provide a straitjacket which restricts the opportunity for change. Managements must use their skills to adapt to change and search out opportunities, as well as threats which can be converted into opportunities, and also weaknesses which can be converted into strengths. It requires far more skill to deal with a turbulent environment than a stable one, and the successful managers are the ones who can deal with change. For example, most managers can be successful in a growing industry but it takes an exceptional manager to be successful in a declining one.

When a business has clear goals, managers need to build an organization with the right people, motivation and controls. In fact, long-term success comes from developing an organization culture which is adaptive to a changing environment (see Box ECM1.1).

BOX ECM1.1

Culture and strategy

In 'Corporate strategists under fire' it was demonstrated that strategy, no matter how good, was inadequate to ensure success.[1]

Corporate culture or personality was perceived to be *the* big stumbling block to implementation, as it was not appropriate or conducive to the overall strategy.[2] The constant methodology, with variations on the theme, is **survey – feedback – plan for change.**

The conclusion of Kiechal's review in *Fortune* is worth quoting:

> For all the hype, culture is real and powerful. It is also hard to change, and you won't find much support for doing so inside or outside your company.

Interestingly, when a culture clash does occur it is suggested that '[you] attempt to dodge: if you must meddle with culture directly, tread carefully and with modest expectations'.

Sources:
1 Kiechal, W. 'Corporate Strategists Under Fire' *Fortune* (27 December 1982).
2 Business Week, 'The corporate culture vultures', *Business Week* (17 October 1983).

Successful businesses have an organization structure which is supportive and is able to keep the business on target. However, the managers normally deal with the problems of reaching the targets set rather than the issues of the future, which require them to address the question of change. In fact success in reaching current goals reinforces 'the way things are done' and makes it harder to deal with change or even to feel a need for it.

It is very difficult for managers both to achieve goals and to adapt to change. This is because managers make decisions, perceive the results and learn from them. Success reinforces the action taken: the better the results, and the more frequent the reinforcement, the more is learned. In this way managers develop guidelines, policies, rules and controls which reinforce the successful behaviour and so make it harder to change. This learning is a powerful guide to success in the environment in which it is acquired, but it is a barrier to change when the environment changes. How many of us work in a stable environment?

There is an in-built resistance to change, as we tend to reject information which threatens our success. The same is true of organizations, since stability is valued because it provides an environment in which goals can be easily attacked.

The signs that change is required often appear gradually and are perceived differently by competitors. Some see the need earlier than others and become successful. In what ways can we get managers and organizations to develop long sight and peripheral vision?

A 'learning organization' not only uses the information from its experience but actively seeks new information, adapts to it and plans for it. It is not reactive but proactive, and this depends on you, the manager.

Change is an inescapable fact of life in any organization and pervades society in general, affecting everybody and every organization up to an international level. An organization can only be successful to the extent that it interacts successfully with its environment. Therefore, the structure and operation of the organization will also reflect the nature of the environment in which it is operating. The organization must be able to respond and adapt to change due to uncertain economic conditions, fierce competition, government interventions, scarce resources and rapid technological innovation.

Change is also occurring within the organization due to ageing, since resources such as buildings or equipment deteriorate, human resources age or skills become outdated. Some of this change can be managed by planned maintenance, new technology or succession planning, and training and development. Other pressures for change come from new strategies or policies, changes in technology, employee attitudes and behaviour. The internal pressures and changes can usually be predicted but the external environment often produces unexpected changes, and these are more difficult to deal with.

Organization change can be a response to new challenges or opportunities presented by the external environment or an anticipation of future problems, such as government regulations or new technology. In some cases the changes may be planned, and this involves modifying the behaviour of people in the organization and improving its ability to cope with change (see **Box ECM1.2**).

BOX ECM1.2

OD: planned change

Concept

Organization development (OD) is a method of facilitating change within the organization to adapt to turbulent external environments. To Bennis it is 'a response to change, a complex educational strategy intended to change the beliefs, attitudes, values and structures of organizations so they can better adapt to new technologies, markets and challenges'.[1]

OD does not just rely on formal training to change people; instead it has a focus on individuals, groups and organizations, and stimulates overall organizational improvement. The concept of teamwork is at the heart of OD, which aims to have a simultaneous development of people and of the organization.

There are clear task objectives but the essence of OD is that nothing can change until behaviour changes. In turn, behavioural change may be linked to attitudes, values and interpersonal relations. In part, the emphasis is on the 'soft' people elements, using conflict resolution methods, effective team management and problem-solving techniques, all underpinned by behavioural research. The 'processes' are usually linked to 'structural' changes as well and a change agent (see Box ECM1.3) is often employed from outside the organization.

Aims

■ OD attempts to improve the **coping mechanisms** within the organization, so that the institution can adopt and adapt to change.

■ A more proactive aim of OD is to create a **climate** where the organization is better able to deal with its existing and its future problems.

■ OD attempts to integrate the human side of enterprise with that of the task. The **socio-technical structures** should be as one.

■ Greater collaboration between sections of the workforce is an aim of OD and this should stimulate **common objectives**.

■ The **processes of getting things done**, from planning to communications and decision making, are emphasized in change programmes.

■ **People** are seen not only as 'inputs' into improved working efficiency, but **as key aspects** of the 'change capacity' within the organization.

So the emphasis is on how the business operates, how its interrelated 'bits' come together, and how we integrate people with the task of facilitating a culture of adaptability and flexibility.

Sources:

1 Bennis, W.G., *Organisation Development: its nature, origins and prospects* (Addison-Wesley, Reading, MA, 1969).

The person or group responsible for the management of the process of change is often called the **change agent**. A change agent can be a group or member of the organization or brought in from outside. For example, outsiders with no vested interests in an organization are more likely to be confided in and listened to and therefore are more likely to make objective judgements (see Box ECM1.3).

BOX ECM1.3

The change agent

Lewin has given us the simple change sequence of:

unfreezing → movement → refreezing.[1]

From the perspective of the change agent this can be a useful methodology. However, the three main phases may have subdivisions in reality.

Diagnosis/assessment
The ostensible difficulty or issue must be investigated. The organization's definition of the problem can be examined at the beginning of the involvement by the change agent. Here it is easier if the catalyst comes from outside the organization, as the consultant or adviser may well be required to wean management away from their 'solution' to their 'problem'. Assessing the potential readiness for change and assessing what the client wants out of the relationship are important aspects of this diagnosis.

Roles and objectives
A role is a pattern of behaviour associated with a position. Both client and consultant may have views on the expected behaviour. These views must be reconciled and some informal, if not formal, agreement of expected processes and outcomes worked out in advance.

Planning and goal setting
The land of the possible must be reached, so careful planning and staged targets can be useful in setting out goals.

Methods
The type of intervention (see later) or method must be consistent with the roles, objectives and milestones – as well as acceptable to both parties – and both valid and reliable as a methodology in its own right.

Relationships
Much of the work will be based on a mutual understanding of what is required. Interpersonal skills can be taxed accordingly. Eventually the relationship will have to be wound down or indeed terminated.

The decision to end any relationship can cause grief to one or both of the parties. Timing can be difficult, but a pull-out situation can be determined by the client's level of confidence and by the change agent's ability to facilitate 'refreezing'.

Sources:

1 Lewin, K., *Field Theory in Social Science* (Harper and Row, New York, 1951).

In spite of the consultant–client relationship seen in Box ECM1.3, it is to some extent part of every manager's job to be a change agent, to be alert to situations and people needing to change, and to be alert to and implement new ideas.

Change in organizations may occur through a **top-down** process starting with the top management. This can be rapid and effective but it may be perceived as insensitive by lower ranks and can be resisted and result in a lack of commitment.

Bottom-up change can start throughout an organization and is essential to organization innovation, adapting operations and technologies. It is particularly strong in creating the competitive advantage of participation.

Successful organizations allow for both top-down and bottom-up change processes to occur.

Managers may respond to pressures for change by denying they exist, resisting them or avoiding them. However, it is much better if managers react to indications of a need for change as it arises or develop a programme of planned change. This may involve a significant investment of time and money to alter the way an organization operates.

The piecemeal approach is part of every manager's job but the planned approach is greater in scope and size and may be dealing with changes which are crucial for survival. Managers should be aware that they cannot predict and respond to all the forces for change in our environment, but they do need to be able to make decisions about priorities. Perhaps managers should accept change and the need to respond to it quickly and plan for it as an important **value** for the organization. This approach views change as necessary to foster the growth of both the organization and the individual.

The effective management of change is an increasingly important responsibility for managers and it must be based on a clear understanding of behaviour at work. People are emotionally involved with their work through their membership of an organization, and they are concerned about the effects of change on their money, security, status, self-esteem and time. Thus change affects each person in a different way and managers must take account of its individual nature.

An alternative vision is demonstrated in Activity ECM1.1. Please tackle the activity and then refer to Box ECM1.4.

We believe that a humanistic philosophy of management which takes account of the task and people needs of an organization (as seen in Box

---

ACTIVITY ECM1.1

AS A CHANGE PROCESS OD IS REDUNDANT

Activity code
- ☑ Self-development
- ☑ Teamwork
- ☑ Communications
- ☐ Numeracy/IT
- ☑ Decisions

Task

Discuss or debate the following:

Management has the upper hand in recessionary times, with pools of unemployed labour and weak trade unions. If change is necessary it can be forced on the workers and it does not need the consensus of liberal-minded OD programmes.

BOX ECM1.4

OD: philosophy and techniques

Open systems
Adherents of OD change programmes see organizations as 'open' or in constant interaction with their external environments. So this open systems approach recognizes the ongoing impact of the external environments on the 'internal environments' of the firm or institution. Like animals, institutions adapt or die. This philosophy necessitates a sound intelligence system and a preparedness to adapt and adopt. It also implies that it is a two-way process between an organization and its external environments.

Human relations

The concepts of trust and openness are inherent in the OD processes. Individual and group needs must be taken into account in the workplace. The philosophy that contented cows give the best milk, held by the proponents of human relations, may be evident in OD, but it seems to be a more humanistic approach than the imposition of forced changes in workforces by diktat from above.

This philosophy uses training, challenging work tasks, job or task restructuring and leadership- or participative-style approaches to gain consensus.

Behavioural sciences

The application of sociology, psychology and OB (organizational behaviour) to the workplace are inherent in the change programmes of OD.

Action research, force field techniques, group learning, interpersonal skills and group dynamics are all examples of such techniques, borrowed from the behavioural sciences.

Task management

OD is not some 'country-club' type of management; it is very much geared to the task requirements of the job. What it does is to fuse the people side with the task side; hence the **socio-technical** influence is strong in this approach.

Techniques such as the grid, managerial effectiveness, audits, task/people requirements of leadership, and mutual goal setting through some variation of management by objectives would come under this heading.

Planned change

The key to OD is the concept of planning. Change occurs in a random fashion and, left to its own devices, can be random in its impact. OD attempts to set forward a plan based upon analysis to cope with change and to bring it about.

ECM1.4) makes for more long-lasting change. This means that the managerial style and the approach to leadership can be key elements of this approach. Of course, planning is critical to the whole change process.

We believe that the aspirations of an educated labour force will demand a higher quality of working life and a part in decision making. However, managerially imposed changes based on product change and technology are clearly becoming more significant as environmental turbulence increases. It is important that managers take these factors into account before taking action, since change may well be resisted.

In recent years, increasing environmental and organizational turbulence has caused many managers to use coercion rather than a humanistic approach to change. At the end of the day, change by diktat can lead to greater resistance and poorer morale, which can destroy the climate of enterprise in the firm. The pressures for change can be appreciated through Activity ECM1.2.

ACTIVITY ECM1.2

PRESSURES FOR CHANGE

Activity code

☑ Self-development
☑ Teamwork
☑ Communications
☑ Numeracy/IT
☑ Decisions

Hellriegal et al.[1] believe that the pressures for change in organizations come from:

■ changing technology

■ the knowledge explosion

■ rapid product obsolescence

■ the changing nature of the workforce

■ the quality of working life

Task

By group or individual initiative, expand on these issues, giving appropriate examples from your country.

Source:

1 D. Hellriegal, J.W. Slocum and R.W. Woodman, *Organisational Behaviour* (West Publishing Co., St Paul, MN, 1989).

C. Change through Looking Back

Nevertheless, being able to adapt to these pressures is not enough. Management must meet the task and people objectives of the business.[2] The vision of enterprise and of continuously improving performance must be related to these changes. Here we emphasize change and enterprise through improved performance on a continuous basis. We turn now to discuss performance.

Grinyer et al.[3] use the criteria in figure ECM1.1. Other criteria are discussed in Unit 6 of *Effective Business Policy*.[4] However, it is a matter not just of measuring performance but of comparing that performance with something else, such as previous performance, a major competitor, a market leader or the industry norms.

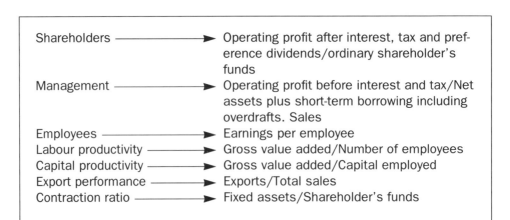

Figure ECM1.1 Criteria for measuring performance.

Source: Adapted from Grinyer, P.H., Mayes, D.G. and McKiernan, P., *Sharpbenders: the secrets of unleashing corporate potential* (Blackwell Publishers, Oxford, 1988).

Whilst every organization has its own acceptable levels of performance in such criteria, those levels may not be the optimum ones. A manager's job is to find those optimum levels. Figure ECM1.2 shows that three levels of performance can be identified for each of the criteria chosen – failure, acceptable and target. Failure indicates the level at which the organization will go out of business. This chart may, therefore, be used as a basis for continuous improvement of performance.

Charts can be kept for each of the criteria and any which fall below acceptable levels need investigating and correcting. On the other hand the various levels may need to be changed each year to reflect inflation, the economic cycle or continuous improvement. Targets must be realistic and achievable and chosen using participation where possible. You should now be able to do Activity ECM1.3.

	Failure	Acceptable	Target
Shareholders			
Management			
Employees			
Labour productivity			
Capital productivity			
Export performance			
Contraction ratio			

Figure ECM1.2 Various levels of performance for an organization.

ACTIVITY ECM1.3

PERFORMANCE CRITERIA

Activity code
☑ Self-development
☐ Teamwork
☑ Communications
☑ Numeracy/IT
☑ Decisions

These are the first of a series of self-developmental tasks related to an organization of your choice. If you are in full-time work, use your existing organization. If you are a student you can use your college or do desk research on a firm of your choice.

Task
1 Identify several criteria for measuring the performance of your organization.
2 Identify target, acceptable and failure levels of performance for each criterion.
3 Find out how your organization performed on the criteria over the last five years. Plot the results on a graph for each criterion, together with what you believed to be the target, acceptable and failure levels of performance for each criterion.
4 What do these graphs tell you?
5 Write a report on your conclusions for 'your' organization.

D. Change through Looking Forwards

Whilst Grinyer et al. based their recommendations for change on the assessment of past experience, Ansoff and McDonnell developed a success hypothesis which stated that a firm's performance is optimized when its aggressiveness and responsiveness match its environment.[5] This has been validated by a number of research studies and should therefore form a good basis on which to proceed.

Ansoff and McDonnell see **environmental turbulence** as a measure of the changeability and predictability of a firm's environment. Changeability is dependent on the complexity of the environment and the familiarity of the challenges to the firm, whereas predictability is a combination of the rapidity of change and the ability to see the future. They identified five levels of turbulence:

Level 1 Environments are repetitive in the sense that the market is stable; the challenges repeat themselves; change is slower than the organization's ability to respond; the future is expected to be the same as the past.

Level 2 Complexity increases but managers can still extrapolate from the past and forecast the future with confidence.

Level 3 Complexity increases further but the organization's response is too slow. The future can still be predicted with some degree of confidence.

Level 4 Turbulence increases with the addition of global and socio-political changes. The future is only partly predictable.

Level 5 Turbulence increases further with unexpected events and situations occurring more quickly than the organization can respond.

Over the years, management systems have been developed to deal with these levels of turbulence. Now complete Activity ECM1.4, which deals with this area.

ACTIVITY ECM1.4

TURBULENCE LEVELS AND MANAGEMENT SYSTEMS

Activity code

- ✓ Self-development
- ☐ Teamwork
- ☐ Communications
- ☐ Numeracy/IT
- ✓ Decisions

The chart shows turbulence levels and management systems.[1]

Environment	Level 1 Repetitive	Level 2 Expanding	Level 3 Changing	Level 4 Discontinuous	Level 5 Surprising
Future	Predictable	Forecastable by extrapolation	Predictable threats and opportunities	Partially predictable opportunities	Unpredictable surprises
Management	By control	By extrapolation	By anticipating change	By flexible and rapid response	Management of surprises
Systems	Policy and procedure manuals	Financial control and capital budgeting	Long range planning	Strategic planning Strategic management	Strategic management Strategic issues Crisis management

Source:
1 Adapted from Ansoff, I.H. and McDonnell, E.J., *Implanting Strategic Management* (Prentice Hall, Englewood Cliffs, NJ, 1990).

Task
1 Think about your 'own' organization and circle the relevant factors in the above figure.
2 What does this tell you about your organization?

Aggressiveness is described by the degree of discontinuity with the past of the firm's new products/services, competitive environments and market strategies; and the timeliness of the introduction of new products and services.

Level 1 is usually only found in not-for-profit organizations, which do not change unless forced by a threat to their survival.
Level 2 is characterized by Henry Ford, who standardized production.
Level 3 organizations are those that shape and influence a customer's needs, perhaps using artificial obsolescence.
Level 4 organizations scan their environment for future opportunities. The aim is to be where the action is by entering and exiting industries.
Level 5 organizations aim to remain at the cutting edge of design and technology.

The **responsiveness** of the firm must also match the environment, and it is described by the climate or management propensity to respond in a particular way – for instance, to welcome, control or reject change; management's competence or ability to respond; and the capacity or the volume of work the management can handle.

Level 1 organizations are change-rejecting, precedence-driven, highly structured, hierarchical and centralized. Management is custodial or control-driven.
Level 2 organizations are efficiency-driven and adapt to change. Power is in the production function. Management is production-driven.
Level 3 organizations are market-driven, extrovert and future-oriented, based on historical strengths. Management is market-driven.
Level 4 organizations are environment-driven. The seat of power is dependent on the challenge. Management is strategy-driven.
Level 5 organizations are environment-creating, may be driven by the market or research and development, and are committed to creativity. Management is by flexible response.

Strategic activities or aggressiveness and operations activities or responsiveness compete for resources and management attention in firms at level 4 and 5.

Systemic resistance to change occurs when:

■ there is a mismatch between aggressiveness and responsiveness;

■ responsiveness lags behind aggressiveness during the change process.

Ansoff and McDonnell provide worksheets for diagnosing the level of turbulence, managers' profiles, management climate profiles and management competence profiles. These are used to diagnose an organization's current and future capability. To appreciate this approach, complete Activity ECM1.5.

ACTIVITY ECM1.5

OPTIMIZING PERFORMANCE

Activity code

☑ Self-development
☐ Teamwork
☐ Communications
☐ Numeracy/IT
☑ Decisions

The chart below and the descriptions of environments, aggressiveness and responsiveness in the text can be used to optimize an organization's performance by comparing its present profile with its required future profile. Steps can then be taken to bring them into line if necessary.

Level	Environment	Aggressiveness	Responsiveness
5	Surprising	Creative	Flexible
4	Discontinuous	Entrepreneurial	Strategic
3	Changing	Anticipatory	Marketing
2	Expanding	Reactive	Production
1	Repetitive	Stable	Custodial

Levels 1, 2 and 3 are largely change-controlling, whereas levels 4 and 5 are change-generating and require different styles of management. Most organizations today will be at levels 4 and 5.

Tasks

1 Identify the current environmental conditions for 'your' organization or one of your choice. Predict the environment in five years and in ten years.

2 Identify the current aggressiveness and responsiveness of 'your' organization. Do these match the current environment? Explain. What has to be done?

3 Do the current aggressiveness and responsiveness match the future environment of 'your' organization? Explain. What has to be done to bring them into line?

Our approach involves a similar interaction between the external environments and the organization. However, instead of having a hierarchy of levels like Ansoff and McDonnell's we suggest that organizations pass through various stages of a relatively 'steady state', decline and growth. This is not suggesting a product life cycle or an ageing or maturation process. It is expressing the view that external environmental factors interact with organizational variables and these three phases occur. The issue for management is how to adapt to or implement these phases. We will pursue these in later units. First we must consider behavioural resistance to change.

E. Behavioural Resistance to Change

Changes which threaten the culture and power of individuals and groups in organizations cause **behavioural resistance**. For example Ansoff and McDonnell[6] found that the level of resistance to change is determined by:

- the degree of discontinuity in the historical culture and power structure implied by the change;
- the length of the period over which the change is introduced;
- the threats, insecurities, loss of prestige and loss of power implied for key individuals;
- the expected contribution by the change to the success or survival of the organization;
- the strength of positive or negative loyalty towards the organization felt by the participants;
- the strength of the cultural and power drives at the respective power centres;
- distorted perception, which can mean that resistance will be higher than is justified by the facts of the situation.

Other types of resistance to change can be seen in Boxes ECM1.5 and ECM1.6. Thereafter complete Activity ECM1.6.

BOX ECM1.5

Resistance to change

In spite of the pressures on organizations to change, it is inevitable that change will be resisted both by people and by organizations. This resistance to change takes many forms and may vary from strikes to subtle reactions which management may never become aware of.

Hellriegal et al.[1] believe that **individual resistance to change** comes from:

- selective attention and retention
- habit

- dependence
- fear of the unknown
- economic reasons
- security and regression

They believe that **organization resistance to change** comes from:
- threats to power and influence
- organization structure
- resource limitations
- fixed investments
- inter-organization agreements

From an employee's perspective, change can be, and often is, threatening. The whole basis of working methods, customs, practices and agreements that have existed for years can be disrupted. Lay-offs and redundancies also have negative effects. The organization needs to counter its own limitations to change, which range from political games to resource limitations.

Source:

1 Adapted from Hellriegal, D., Slocum, J.W. and Woodman, R.W., *Organisational Behaviour* (West Publishing Co., St Paul, MN, 1989).

BOX ECM1.6

Social resistance

The problems of implementing change normally centre on the technical and financial aspects of change in the early stages. The organization and social aspects are left until later. However, a manager should begin to think about implementation at the very outset of considering change because the organization and social aspects are just as critical – if not more so.

The introduction of change involves people and the social system. Unless managers can introduce change in such a way that people will accept and support it then the change will not be successful. Social change is a major part of the change process in any organization and needs just as much effort as the changes in finance, administration or technology which managers are used to coping with.

We develop this approach in the main text.

ACTIVITY ECM1.6

CHANGE: A STAKEHOLDER APPROACH

Activity code
☑ Self-development
☐ Teamwork
☑ Communications
☐ Numeracy/IT
☑ Decisions

Task

Consider 'your' organization.[1]

1 Identify the stakeholders and their motivating interests, attitudes and likely reactions to change.

2 In order to assess support for a particular change, identify the stakeholders and assign them each a weight from 1 to 10 to indicate their importance to implementing the change. If the change can be made without the involvement of the stakeholder, then the weight is 1. If the change cannot be carried out without the involvement of the stakeholder, then the weight is 10.

3 Now score the attitude of each stakeholder towards the expected results of change, from 'active resistance' = 1 to 'enthusiastic support' = 10.

4 Multiply the importance weights by the attitude weights in order to determine the importance of the stakeholder to the change process. Important stakeholders who are resistant need special attention. Therefore, an analysis of the causes of the resistance may be required.

5 Identify the social resources you have available for implementing the change. Social resources are characteristics of each stakeholder, such as friendships, loyalties, habits, perceptions, psychological style, anxieties, prejudices, shared beliefs, identification with purpose, will power and dedication.

6 Finally, write a short report on the social change problem. What are the social barriers to change and in what ways can they be overcome?

Source:
1 Adapted from Rowe, A.J., Mason, R.O., Dickel, K.E. and Synder, N.H., *Strategic Management: a methodological approach* (Addison-Wesley, Reading, MA, 1990).

We will now develop the social aspect of change as it impacts upon the key stakeholders in change – the employees. Our view is that the overriding philosophy of management towards the concept of change is linked to management treatment of its employees. In turn, these philosophies and employee relationships will impact on the degree of resistance to change.

A useful classification of employee relationship styles of management can be seen in Box ECM1.7.

BOX ECM1.7

A question of style

The interesting work of Purcell and Sisson,[1] building on the earlier work of Fox,[2] noted the following types of style in management–employee relationships:

Traditional	An authoritarian approach to staff. Clearly anti-union and opposed to recognizing unions. Perhaps latter-day unitarists.
Classical conflict //	Unions are here but perhaps management could live without them. Constant challenge from unions, and conflict predominates between managers and unions.
Sophisticated moderns	A more subtle managerial approach: unions are here so we need to accept and involve them. Effective communications and consent are important to 'break down the barriers'. This aims at getting the workers 'on management's side' and is an indirect form of control.
Continuous challenge	A conflict zone. Workgroup controls clash with managerial prerogatives in this battle for dominance.
Sophisticated paternalists	Unions are not normally seen as 'necessary'. The good employer looks after the interests of the workers through 'progressive' personnel policies. Management pursues its objectives in an unfettered manner. This looks like a human resources management (HRM) variation.[3]

Sources:

1 Purcell, J. and Sisson, K., 'Strategies and practice in the management of industrial relations', in *Industrial Relations in Britain*, ed. C.S. Bain (Blackwell Publishers, Oxford, 1983).

2 Fox, A., 'Industrial sociology and industrial relations', RCTUEA Research Paper 3 (HMSO, London, 1966).

3 Anderson, A.H., *Effective Personnel Management* (Blackwell Publishers, Oxford, 1994).

These philosophies will impact on change and its management. See figure ECM1.3.

So the 'organization development' frame of reference or the pluralistic view of the 'sophisticated moderns' is seen to be the way forward in change management.

On the other hand, Kotter and Schlesinger's classification[7] can also help our understanding. These writers identify a range of methods to overcome change such as:

1 coercion

2 manipulation

3 education

4 support

Managerial philosophy style	Implication for change
Traditional	Management is by diktat, and trade unions and employees are told of the changes. Little consensus occurs.
Classical conflict	It is difficult to introduce change here as management and labour are at odds with one another. Change may be forced through, but open resistance will occur.
Sophisticated moderns	The views of others are accepted, so negotiation, discussion and agreement to change are likely.
Continuous challenge	Change may be introduced on paper but informal controls and negotiation on a daily basis between management and workers will mean that the change does not really take place.
Sophisticated paternalists	This is a canny approach by management. It lends itself to consensus, as management is seen as liberal in this 'human resources' approach to change.

Figure ECM1.3 Managerial philosophies and the implications for change.

5 participation

6 negotiation

In our view, (1) and (2) are not acceptable while (3) to (6) are seen as the way forward for change management. We develop these ideas in the next section.

F. Overcoming Resistance to Change

Even if a liberal style of management prevails, change upsets the status quo, so some resistance is likely.

Ansoff and McDonnell[8] see change as impacting on two areas: systems (structures, skills and knowledge) and behaviour (culture, norms, perceptions, values, beliefs, attitudes and power). The way to produce the maximum resistance when introducing change is as follows:

1 Introduce the change.

2 Alter the systems to suit. This triggers behavioural resistance, which is often interpreted as a systemic deficiency. This is corrected, triggering more behavioural resistance, and so on.

3 Eventually either the behaviour gradually changes or the change is abandoned.

Thus the

Change $\rightarrow$ Systems $\rightarrow$ Behaviour

approach is the maximum resistance sequence.

The way to minimize resistance when introducing change is as follows:

1 Make the behaviour change.

2 Introduce systems.

3 Consolidate behaviour.

However, if you make the behavioural changes first, followed by the systemic changes, then the change required can be put in place with the minimum of resistance. Thus:

Behaviour $\rightarrow$ Systems $\rightarrow$ Change = Success

According to Kotter and Schlesinger,[9] resistance to change can be overcome by the following actions:

■ **Education and communication** when there is a lack of information or inaccurate information and analysis. This involves explaining the need for and logic of change to individuals, groups and even the entire organization.

■ **Participation and involvement** when the initiators do not have all the information they need to design the change, and others have considerable power to resist. This involves asking members of the organization to help design the change.

■ **Facilitation and support** when people are resisting because of adjustment problems. This involves offering retraining programmes, time off, emotional support and understanding to people affected by the change.

■ **Negotiation and agreement** when some person or group, with considerable power to resist, will clearly lose out on a change. This involves negotiating with potential resisters, and even soliciting written letters of understanding.

■ **Manipulation and co-operation** when other tactics will not work, or are too expensive. This involves giving key persons a desirable role in designing or implementing the change process.

■ **Explicit and implicit coercion** when speed is essential and the change initiators possess considerable power. This involves threatening job loss or transfer, lack of promotion, etc.

Our views on the last two approaches have been mentioned earlier.

Lewin[10] developed a way of looking at change called **force field analysis**, which envisages change as a dynamic balance of forces working in opposite directions at any particular point in time. This would mean that any situation is in a state of equilibrium as a result of forces pushing against one another. To Lewin, the forces pushing for change are balanced by forces resisting change (see figure ECM1.4). Thus in order to make a change a manager has to modify the current balance of forces by:

■ increasing the pressure for change;

■ reducing or removing the resisting forces;

■ changing the direction of the force.

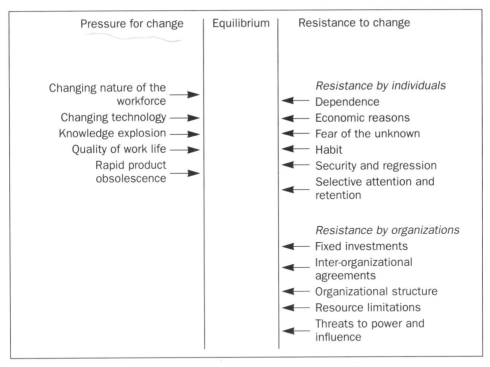

Figure ECM1.4 Pressures for and resistance to change in a force field diagram.

Source: Adapted from Lewin, K., *Field Theory in Social Science* (Harper and Row, New York, 1951).

You can practice using Lewin's force field analysis by completing Activity ECM1.7.

ACTIVITY ECM1.7

FORCES FOR AND RESISTANT TO CHANGE

Activity code

✓ Self-development
✓ Teamwork
☐ Communications
☐ Numeracy/IT
✓ Decisions

Task

Using Lewin's analysis, outline typical forces for change and possible forces which may resist changes in an organization.

It is clear that there are many forces for and against change and it is necessary for managers to identify the key forces in their organization.

The natural tendency for a manager who wants change is to push and for those being pushed to push back. Therefore a more effective way to encourage change is to reduce the existing forces if you can.

This model enables managers to understand the current situation and work out the factors that can or cannot be changed. For instance, any management problem can be analysed into pressures for or against the problem. The pressures for or against change may not be the same as those indicated in figure ECM1.4, but you should be able to insert your own forces on such a force field diagram. The diagram can be improved by indicating the strength of each factor involved, perhaps by the length of a line.

The major difficulty with this concept is the fact that it identifies the situation at a particular point in time. At other times the balance may be different. Also, each person who constructs such a figure may interpret the situation differently. However, provided managers are aware of these difficulties, force field analysis can be a useful management tool.

This approach emphasizes that we should look for multiple causes of behaviour and the forces can be of many types. The behaviour of people, groups or organizations can be assessed. Programmes for planned change can be directed towards removing or weakening the resisting forces and creating or strengthening the driving forces in organizations.

People resist change when they defend something they believe is important to them. Perhaps resistance can be thought of as a form of feedback, which managers should use, for instance, to modify the planned change. In other words, the manager should try to find a better fit between the planned change, the situation and the people involved.

Now read Box ECM1.8, which illustrates the difficulties in change policy. Then you may complete Activity ECM1.8.

BOX ECM1.8

Lorange on trends and constraints

Lorange[1] identified five major trends in the environment which must be addressed during the implementation of change:

1 attitudes
2 politics
3 power shifts
4 scarcity
5 technology

Lorange also identified five constraints within organizations which have to be addressed:

1 executive obsolescence
2 inflexibility
3 parochialism
4 power
5 values, styles, traditions

Source:

1 Adapted from Lorange, P., 'Where do we go from here?: implementation challenges for the 1980s', in *Implementation of Strategic Planning* (Prentice Hall, Englewood Cliffs, NJ, 1982).

ACTIVITY ECM1.8

CONSTRAINTS ON CHANGE

Activity code

- ✓ Self-development
- ☐ Teamwork
- ☐ Communications
- ☐ Numeracy/IT
- ✓ Decisions

Task

1 Make a force field analysis of 'your' organization. Discuss your conclusions.
2 Discuss Lorange's five major trends and their effect on 'your' organization.
3 Discuss Lorange's five major constraints and their effect on 'your' organization.

G. Managing Change

Organization change involves changing the behaviour of people and this focuses on participation and teamwork. Thus the challenge for any organization today is to manage change effectively, since failure to change successfully will rapidly threaten its ability to survive. This applies to both profit and not-for-profit organizations.

There is a difference, of course, between change which is planned and that which is unplanned. In this book we are largely concerned with planned change, namely that set of activities which change people, groups and the organization's processes and structure. This kind of change requires specific objectives which improve the organization's ability to adapt to change and also to facilitate change in employee behaviour.

All parts of the organization are involved in becoming more adaptive, and therefore organization culture has an important influence on organization adaptability. In spite of the difficulties in changing organization culture (see Box ECM1.1), the personality of the organization has an important influence on organizational adaptability.

Managers deal with change in different ways. For instance, they may react to indications that change is needed and deal with problems as they arise. They may also develop a programme of planned change. However, managers today should not only plan for change but accept that change is necessary for the organization to learn, survive and be successful.

In any change situation, as we noted earlier, a person or group should be the catalyst for change or the **change agent** – the leader responsible for managing the change. Change agents may be internal or external. External change agents, such as consultants, bring in extra expertise, and may be confided in, listened to and able to make objective decisions more than internal change agents. If resistance to change is expected to be high, the prestige of the external change agent may be necessary for obtaining agreement and commitment to the proposed changes.

The management of change can be seen at the structural or process level, or a more holistic view can be taken. The structural and process levels can be seen in Box ECM1.9.

BOX ECM1.9

Change: structure and process

Leavitt believes an organization can be changed by altering its structure, technology and/or people.[1] Altering the structure and technology changes the work situation, whereas people approaches change the behaviour of employees.

Changing structure can involve three approaches:

1 **Classical organization design** uses job responsibilities, division of labour and lines of authority to improve organization performance. Managers can change these to improve the performance of their organization.

2 **Decentralization** enables each unit to adapt its structure and technology to the tasks it performs and to its external environment. It places decision making and responsibility closer to the customer and creates smaller, self-contained units which focus on high-priority work activities.

3 The **flow of work** can be modified to improve production and produce higher morale and work satisfaction.

Technological changes are often difficult to implement successfully, since they may be incompatible with the structure of the organization. This fact led to **socio-technological approaches** – small work groups, job enrichment and job enlargement.

People approaches change the behaviour of people by focusing on their attitudes, expectations, perceptions and skills. This should lead to better job performance and to employee-initiated changes in other areas, such as structure and technology.

Ansoff and McDonnell propose building a launching platform for the change.[2] This consists of:

- minimizing the start-up resistance;
- marshalling a power base sufficient to give the change momentum and continuity;
- preparing a detailed plan for the change process which assigns responsibilities, resources, steps and interactions through which the change will be carried out;
- designing into the plan behavioural features which optimize acceptance and support for the change.

A supportive climate can be developed by:

- discussing the change openly;
- eliminating or reducing fears;
- producing a pro-change power base by:
  - changing the power structure;
  - forming a coalition of those who will benefit and persuading luke-warm supporters;
  - offering rewards for support;
  - neutralizing potential resistance by bargaining, for instance.

Sources:

1 Adapted from Leavitt, H.J., 'Applied organisation change in industry: structural, technological and human approaches', in *New Perspectives in Organisation Research*, eds W. Cooper, H.J. Leavitt and M.W. Shelly (Wiley, New York, 1964).
2 Ansoff, I.H. and McDonnell, E.J., *Implanting Strategic Management* (Prentice Hall, Englewood Cliffs, NJ, 1990).

Lewin[11] gives us a more holistic approach with three phases for planned organization change:

1 **Unfreezing** – Managers must create a **need** for change by:
   - establishing a good relationship with the people involved;
   - helping people realize present behaviour is not effective;
   - minimizing resistance to change.

In order for change to be successful, Lewin believes an organization must be ready for it.

2 **Changing** – managers must **implement** change by:
   - identifying more effective behaviour;
   - choosing appropriate changes in tasks, culture, technology and structure;

– taking action.

Lewin believes many managers enter the changing phase too early and therefore end up creating resistance to change. There is also a greater chance of failure in this way.

3 **Refreezing** – managers must **stabilize** the change by:
   – creating acceptance and continuity for the new behaviour;
   – providing support;
   – using performance-contingent rewards and positive reinforcement.

Lewin believes it is also important to evaluate results, provide feedback and make any necessary modifications.

Whatever approach we use, perhaps there are general principles of managing change (see Box ECM1.10) which can apply (see also Activity ECM1.9).

BOX ECM1.10

General principles for managing change

Mullins provides the following general principles for the management of change:[1]

- An environment of trust and shared commitment should be created by involving staff in decisions and actions which affect them. Indeed, the Employment Act 1982 requires all companies with over 250 employees to report annually on the steps taken to introduce, maintain or develop arrangements for employee consultation and involvement, information sharing, employee share schemes and related matters.

- There should be full and genuine participation of all the staff concerned well before the introduction of change. Staff should be actively encouraged to contribute their own ideas, suggestions and experiences and to voice openly their worries and concerns.

- Team management, a co-operative spirit among staff and workers, and a genuine feeling of shared involvement will create a greater willingness to accept change. A participative style of management and management by objectives (MbO) are useful approaches.

- The introduction of incentive schemes may help in motivating people by an equitable allocation of savings which result from change.

- Changes to the work organization must maintain the balance to the socio-technical system. New working practices must take into account how best to satisfy the needs and expectations of people at work through the practical application of behavioural science.

- Careful attention should be given to job design, methods of working, the development of cohesive groups, and relationships between the nature and content of jobs and their task functions.

Source:
1 Adapted from Mullins, L.J., 'Information technology – the human factor', *Administrator*, 5 (1985), pp. 6–9.

ACTIVITY ECM1.9

CHANGE AT THE PAPER MILL

Activity code
✓ Self-development
☐ Teamwork
☐ Communications
☐ Numeracy/IT
✓ Decisions

The Paper Mill was experiencing difficult market conditions, particularly as much of the board market had taken a sharp fall as a result of the recession in the building industry.

A decision was taken by senior management to invest in their staff and in new plant. Cost benefits would result and the firm would be able to bid more competitively (that is, more cheaply) for the work available in the building sector.

New machines were introduced and a new employee/labour relations package was floated with the unions in the plant.

Senior management expected structural and attitudinal change to accompany the new technology. The grading structure was changed to give greater flexibility between jobs and to give employees more opportunity to progress through the structure. A new job evaluation system was introduced. The various sick-pay and holiday schemes were harmonized so that white- and blue-collar differentials and differences became a thing of the past. Job role not collar colour determined the level of pay. Wages were moved to direct credit transfer, so all employees were now of salaried status.

The removal of these artificial barriers was welcomed, as were the training initiatives. Change awareness training, teamwork and culture awareness development, and skills training for the multiskilling process all took place.

Communication processes were revamped. Brochures, a monthly newsletter, ongoing discussion groups on the shop floor, and negotiation and consultation meetings took place with the trade unions.

The excess jobs were negotiated out through enhanced payments and through voluntary redundancy or early retirement programmes. A consultancy firm specializing in out-placement and counselling was brought in to ease any pain. The personnel department co-ordinated the whole scheme.

So a more cohesive work group, more supportive of one another and far more flexible than before, was now in place. The employees who remained were more highly paid and most had career routes through reskilling. The new technology was in place and in operation. Overall costs were tumbling but the competitive environment was becoming even harder. Compulsory redundancies were on the horizon.

Task
Critically appraise the management and leadership involved in this change process.

From the general principles outlined by Mullins (Box ECM1.10) we can turn to more specific principles and then to techniques. We will conclude this unit by applying an OD approach to these principles and techniques through an activity and reinforcing our approach to change and enterprise, which we will follow throughout the book.

H. Change and Decision Making

Diesing suggested that three principles should be used to select a change from a series of options and the process repeated if necessary to reach a solution for social change:[12]

1 The **principle of changeability**: select the easiest possible relevant changes within the business.

The ease of change is based on the concepts of **introducibility** and **acceptability**.

Introducibility depends on roles being in place in the social system that will allow the changes to occur. Also, managers or employees must have sufficient skill to perform those roles effectively. If roles have to be changed in order to make progress then the people who have to change must be won over.

Acceptability involves more than gaining the approval of stakeholders. The change must be made with the minimum of disruption, incompatibility and conflict. Thus, change is more likely to be accepted if it is similar to the situation it replaces, and small changes are more likely to be acceptable than large changes.

2 The **principle of separability**: select a change that is sufficiently isolated from its context for it to be implemented while protected from outside pressures.

3 The **principle of growth**: begin a change in such a way that extension of change is possible.

Where should the seed operation be started? What social relationships can be changed so that a chain reaction is triggered in the right direction?

Often, changes in a few activities and interactions lead to changes in sentiments and norms. This reinforces the changes and permits new activities to be started and the process repeated. During each iteration the target area is increased in size and complexity.

It may well be that targets for change may not satisfy all three principles. In that case the options should be re-examined until one is found that introduces change easily, is easy to separate and will trigger a chain reaction.

Please read Box ECM1.11 and complete Activity ECM1.10, which concludes this unit.

BOX ECM1.11

Change techniques

The Harris Research Group, on behalf of KPMG Consultants, examined some 250 responses from senior managers concerned with change.[1] The findings on the techniques being used, reported in October 1993, make interesting reading:

- Seventy per cent used total quality management (TQM) and customer care programmes.
- Employee empowerment was used by 61 per cent.
- Sixty-four per cent used performance measurement.
- Business process redesign or re-engineering was being used by 52 per cent.
- Forty-eight per cent used cultural change.
- Activity-based measurement was used by 40 per cent.

Source:
1 *Management Consultants News*, 4(12), 1993.

ACTIVITY ECM1.10

SUCCESSFUL INTERVENTIONS

Activity code
- ✓ Self-development
- ✓ Teamwork
- ☐ Communications
- ☐ Numeracy/IT
- ✓ Decisions

Task

How would you or your group:
1 isolate the variables with the potential to restrict OD interventions or their success?
2 establish some preconditions for success (excluding the lifting of the identified restrictions)?

Notes

1 Jeans, M., 'Change is the major challenge for business', *Management Consultants News*, 4(12), 1993.

2 See Anderson, A.H., *Effective General Management* (Blackwell Publishers, Oxford, forthcoming).

3 This section is based on Grinyer, P.H., Mayes D.G. and McKiernan, P., *Sharpbenders: the secrets of unleashing corporate potential* (Blackwell Publishers, Oxford, 1988).

4 See Anderson, A.H. and Barker, D., *Effective Business Policy* (Blackwell Publishers, Oxford, 1994).

5 Grinyer et al., *Sharpbenders*. This section also draws upon Ansoff, I.H. and McDonnell, E.J., *Implanting Strategic Management* (Prentice Hall, Englewood Cliffs, NJ, 1990).

6 Ansoff and McDonnell, *Implanting Strategic Management*.

7 Kotter, J.P. and Schlesinger, L.A., 'Choosing strategies for change', *Harvard Business Review*, March/April (1979).

8 Ansoff and McDonnell, *Implanting Strategic Management*.

9 Kotter and Schlesinger, 'Choosing strategies for change'.

10 Lewin, K., *Field Theory in Social Science* (Harper and Row, New York, 1951).

11 Lewin, K., 'Frontiers in group dynamics: concept, method and reality in social science', *Human Relations*, 1(1947), pp. 5–41.

12 Diesing, P., *Reason in Society* (Greenwood Press, Westport, CT, 1962).

ECM Unit Two

Understanding the External Environment

Learning Objectives

After completing this unit you should be able to:

- make a PEST analysis of your organization and identify the key opportunities and threats;
- identify the critical internal and external stakeholders;
- use the necessary generic strategies for dealing with stakeholders;
- identify who and where your customers are and what they want;
- understand the concepts of product, product mix and product life cycle;
- understand and use the concepts of market and marketing mix in order to make market and product assessments;
- make a report on your industry and its competitive environment;
- apply the generic skills.

Contents

A. Overview

B. The External Environment

C. Stakeholders

D. Generic Strategies for Dealing with Stakeholders

E. The Competitive Environment

► The customer

► The product

► The market

F. Market and Product Assessment

G. Industry and the Competitive Environment

► Dominant economic characteristics

► Industry driving forces

► The strength of competitive forces

► The competitive positions of competitors

► Predicting competitors' moves

► Key success factors

► Industry proposals and overall attractiveness.

ECM Unit Two

> ❝ A powerful force drives the world toward a converging common-
> ality, and that force is technology. It has proletarianized com-
> munication, transport and travel . . . The result is a new com-
> mercial reality – the emergence of global markets for
> standardised consumer products on a previously unimagined
> scale of magnitude. ❞
>
> *T. Levitt* [1]

A. Overview

Change tends to emanate from outside the organization, although, of course, internal organizational change from new styles of management to specific policies impact on this process. How the organization reacts and acts towards change or anticipated change is a key aspect of effective enterprise management.

The **macro environments** incorporate political, economic, social and technological aspects. When these change, they can be threatening, or they can energize the organization, depending on their nature and on how they interact with the culture of enterprise within the firm – assuming some personality of enterprise in the organization.

The **micro environments** concern the industry structure, the customers or potential customers, and the external stakeholders and their aspirations. Arguably suppliers and the possibility of substitute products or similar services also fall into this classification. Micro environments can be life threatening or on a par with winning a major state lottery.

The external environments not only facilitate or trigger change but give us opportunities and threats. Opportunity maximization in line with the theme of enterprise, rather than threat minimization, is pursued in this unit. (Threat handling strategies can be seen in *Effective Business Policy* in this series.)[2] Managing the often diverse interests of different stakeholders is all part of this outward vision of managers who look to the external environments.

However, here we argue that understanding competitive environments, the assessment of the marketplace and that of the industrial context are all key aspects of enterprise management and opportunity seeking. Changes tend to be inherent in these environments so enterprise must be fluid in order to adapt and adopt. This 'fluidity' in the organization is pursued in the next unit.

B. The External Environment

The external environment in which an organization operates can be considered under four major headings: **p**olitical, **e**conomic, **s**ociological and **t**echnological (**PEST**). Managers should examine the ways in which each of these influence the organization. The level of detail to which this is taken will depend on the resources available and the ability to make sense of the data collected. However, simply keeping an eye on a few key factors will enable the manager to identify opportunities and threats to the organization. Box ECM2.1 provides an example of how the external environment can impact on a highly developed country.

BOX ECM2.1

PEST: an example

The macro environments are divided up in the text for the sake of analysis only: in reality they merge if not converge. The recent exchange-rate mechanism (ERM) débâcle is illustrative.[1]

The high-speed technology of the speculators facilitates cross-border transactions at the blink of an eye. The political desire to hang on to a system which favoured some mainland European countries at the expense of others because it was 'policy' seems to have been fatally flawed. Linking the pound to the DM at 2.95 inside the ERM and striving for zero inflation through using this mechanism meant credibility suffered, particularly when interest rates tumbled. Britain fell out of the ERM, and wholesale devaluation occurred. Social distress and high unemployment figures, linked to the lack of credibility of a government which was seen as not to be trusted, led opposition parties to speak of a 'government (losing) control of economic policy' (John Smith) and of 'the people [finding] they can no longer trust the solemn words of our leaders, that the Prime Minister's pledges are worthless, that the Chancellor is a man of straw: small wonder they feel betrayed' (Paddy Ashdown).[1]

Source:

1 Adapted from the *Guardian*, 'Economy in crisis', 18 September (1992).

The **political environment** consists of the factors related to the use and/or allocation of power. It is relevant at several levels, local, national and international, and is tempered by special interest groups and other political entities. This environment is supported by the legal and judicial framework of the societies in which the organization operates.

The **economic environment** includes all the factors related to the flow of energy, information, money, products and services. It is obviously critical to the success of the organization. There are two types of economic change which are important to managers: structural and cyclical. **Structural** changes challenge our basic assumptions about how the economy works. Sudden changes in energy costs or a shift from an industrial to a service economy are examples. Such changes may be permanent or temporary. **Cyclical** changes are periodic swings in economic activity such as interest rates and inflation. Structural changes often necessitate a fundamental rethinking of strategies for organizations, whereas cyclical changes are a function of the normal economic climate.

The **sociological environment** includes the factors that affect the way people live, and is produced by three variables: demography, lifestyle and social values. Both the demographic and lifestyle variables will influence the composition, expectations and whereabouts of the organization's labour supply and customers, whereas social values determine the choices people make in life and how managers and organizations operate. Our values change and adjust over time so that policies acceptable a few years ago may not be acceptable today. Moreover, one country's values may not be compatible with those of another. Variations in values may also explain differences between one sector of a population and another.

The **technological environment** is related to the development of knowledge about machines, materials, processes and tools. It is based on advances in science, new materials, products and processes. The level of technology in an organization, industry or society determines the kinds of product and service which can be produced, the equipment used and the methods of management required.

Technology can be a driving force shaping the future of an organization and therefore a way of gaining competitive advantage. On the other hand, failure to recognize new technology can result in an organization failing to survive. Of course, the key environmental issues for one organization will not be the same as another's, even in the same industry.

Box ECM2.2 emphasizes that the internal adoption of technology can be very problematic – even assuming that the environmental issues are understood.

BOX ECM2.2

Managing changing technology

Eason focuses on the spread, or the lack of spread, of new technology.[1] The knowledge exists in the external environment but the internal environments of many firms seem to be slow to embrace it. To Eason, the key is education and there is a need to upgrade and update computer literacy.

The organization is a socio-technical system.[2] According to the HUSAT Research Group at Loughborough University, of which Eason is a member, the problem is that there is a misfit between the social and the technological aspects of IT. The systems are designed by specialists for laypeople. Technology prevails over social considerations. The customers' needs are not fully taken into account at the design stage, so when and if things go wrong, customer needs lead to an amelioration of the impact of the system rather than a rethink of the whole system *per se*.

A more evolutionary approach to introduction, with closer customer involvement and ongoing learning, is seen as the way forward to exploit new technology fully for the enterprising organization.

Sources:

1 Eason, K.D., 'The process of introducing information technology', *Behaviour and Information Technology*, 1(2), 1982.
2 See Anderson, A.H. and Kyprianou, A., *Effective Organizational Behaviour* (Blackwell Publishers, Oxford, 1995).

If relearning is important, as suggested in Box ECM2.2, unlearning may have equal relevance. We tend to perpetuate our past actions. There is a strong incentive to repeat that which worked in the past, to do it better and more efficiently and to get more people to do the same. This is because organizations reinforce successful behaviour by creating information and learning systems, incentives and organization structures around it. However, this approach can have disadvantages, since it can continue to push the organization in the same direction long after the need for it has gone (as in the case of Henry Ford and the Model T).

Please tackle Activity ECM2.1.

ACTIVITY ECM2.1

PEST

Activity code
☑ Self-development
☑ Teamwork
☑ Communications
☐ Numeracy/IT
☑ Decisions

Task

1 Make a PEST analysis for 'your' work organization or college. What changes do you expect in the next five years? And in the next ten years?
2 The climate or environmental factors (PEST) should also be assessed as to their importance and impact. A chart can be produced for each environmental factor – political, environmental, sociological and technological – in order to assist management decision making.

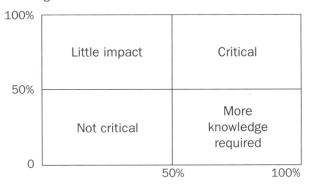

Discuss the importance and impact of the environmental factors. Use a report format (1,000 words maximum).

C. Stakeholders

Stakeholders are those groups or individuals affected directly or indirectly by a firm's pursuit of its goals. Managers have to deal with stakeholders and so balance the conflicting claims on the organization. The competing claims of customers, shareholders, workers and the local community, for instance, have to be assessed in order for the organization to survive. It does not matter whether you are a chief executive officer (CEO) or a first-line manager, you can still make use of the framework which follows.

The external environment of an organization is continually changing and the forces involved create groups or individuals that become stakeholders. Stakeholders are of two types: **internal** and **external** (see figure ECM2.1).

Internal stakeholders	External stakeholders
Employees	Customers
Owners/shareholders	Competitors
Board of directors	Governments
	Suppliers
	Unions
	Financial institutions
	Local community and wider public
	Special interest groups
	Multiple stakeholders

Figure ECM2.1 Typical stakeholders.

In the next unit we discuss the internal stakeholders under our internal analysis. Here we shall focus on the external bodies.

There are many different external stakeholders, the most important of which are the **customers**. Who are they? Where are they? What do they want? How can it be provided at the right price? In what ways can the number of customers be increased? These are just some of the questions which need to be answered.

High quality standards, customer service and the influence of new technology in the form of communications and transportation have made the concept of the 'world' rather than the 'national' product possible. Therefore international customers may need to be catered for.

Dissatisfied customers either take their custom away or complain. **Customer loyalty** will tend to decide whether a firm is successful or not. This is the reason for the importance of brand names and brand loyalty. Complaints should lead to the improvement of the product or service, whereas the loss of a customer can be part of a downward spiral.

Within the organization itself everyone is a customer of everyone else, and this has wide-ranging effects when one considers customer service.

In order to sell its products or services an organization must gain more customers and so must compete against others. Therefore **competitors** are important stakeholders. Competitors are not normally thought of as stakeholders but, in our opinion, they have a stake in your business because their success is dependent on what you do. Therefore they will do everything they can to influence the decisions you make and gain your customers.

Competition does not necessarily mean forcing competitors out of business. This may produce new, even stronger competitors or, even worse, customers may change to substitute products. Therefore, managers should normally think about competition rather than conflict.

A manager must provide superior customer satisfaction in order to beat the competition. Who are your competitors now and could be your competitors in the future? Many firms have disappeared because a competitor appeared unexpectedly and they were unable to respond quickly enough. Foreign competition, laws and cultures may require additional resources to assess competition properly.

The mention of competition above leads on to the place of **governments** as stakeholders. They act as watchdogs, regulating business and industry in the public interest and to ensure market principles are followed. Governments shape an organization's strategy by the way they control financial, fiscal and legal policies. Managers have to deal with local, national and international controls for employment, health, laws, resources, safety and taxes, amongst others.

Consideration of the resources for your business will identify **suppliers** as stakeholders. Suppliers provide energy, equipment, finance, labour, raw materials and services to the organization, which then uses them to produce products and services. Therefore, organizations are dependent on their suppliers in order to survive. Sources of supply need to be kept under constant observation in order to detect potential threats or opportunities.

Managers must look for a competitive edge and this could be in better and/or cheaper supply lines. Quality and standards are important, as also are shortages, poor delivery times and fluctuating prices. The place of stock in the organization must also be examined in detail and a policy developed to optimize its effect on the organization. This may involve capital investment. The effect of new technology in terms of computer control and robots has produced significant changes in this area in recent years.

The need for supplies of labour brings into focus the **unions** as major stakeholders. There have been major changes in labour relations in recent years due to changes in the environment and other stakeholders. Unions are becoming more interested in the quality of life and work. Confrontation is beginning to be avoided in order for firms to be able to survive in the turbulent environment.

The turbulent environment demands the help of **financial institutions**, which are therefore major stakeholders in many organizations. Changes have occurred in the financial markets in recent years and many new products and services have been developed to meet the needs of international trade. The place of new technology has also allowed the trading of stocks, shares and money twenty-four hours per day and instant access to the money situation both inside and outside the organization.

The new mass communication technologies have enabled the media to open organizations to the scrutiny of the **local community and the wider public**. The visual impact of television and investigative reporting are causing managers to become more aware of the impact of their decisions on society. New skills are having to be cultivated in order to deal with public relations and minimize the damage of unforeseen occurrences (for example, Perrier Water and the benzene scare).

These unforeseen occurrences and the needs of society, which develop out of the climate of the environment, have led to the growth of **special interest groups**. Consumer and ecological groups and those with special health, safety and moral interests all have a stake in one organization or another.

Each organization has to satisfy its own unique set of stakeholders, so it is important for managers to identify and prioritize their stakeholders regularly. At the same time, there is a complex network of relationships and coalitions between stakeholders, which also varies from time to time. For instance, employees, unions and ecology groups could unite against a proposed innovation which could cause pollution in one form or another. These **multiple stakeholders** may also develop and change over time.

Please tackle Activity ECM2.2.

ACTIVITY ECM2.2

STAKEHOLDERS I

Activity code
- ✓ Self-development
- ✓ Teamwork
- ✓ Communications
- ☐ Numeracy/IT
- ✓ Decisions

Task

Replace the stakeholders in the chart below with those for your work organization or college. Tick the boxes for those which are related in any way.

	1	2	3	4	5	6	7	8
1 Employees								
2 Owners/shareholders								
3 Board of directors								
4 Competitors								
5 Customers								
6 Regulators								
7 Special interest groups								
8 Suppliers								

Actions taken by one stakeholder or coalition may affect other stakeholders. Over time, stakeholder relationships become more complex and produce a need for new, faster, more reliable responses and better ways of predicting their effects. All stakeholders are affected by the opportunities and threats generated by these responses. The complexity causes the relationships to become more impersonal.

Rowe et al.[3] believe that the success of any organization depends on the validity of the assumptions made about its stakeholders, particularly about how they will respond as the strategy unfolds. To identify and validate the assumptions made about each stakeholder we have to identify these assumptions and rank them with respect to their importance and certainty. Please tackle Activity ECM2.3. Box ECM2.3 gives some assumptions some stakeholders make about a leading UK business.

ACTIVITY ECM2.3

STAKEHOLDERS II

Activity code
- ✓ Self-development
- ☐ Teamwork
- ✓ Communications
- ☐ Numeracy/IT
- ✓ Decisions

Task

Describe each of the stakeholder groups in detail for 'your' organization and then compare each stakeholder group with every other group. Discuss the ways they interact. (Refer back to Activity ECM2.2 and use the type of matrix shown there.)

BOX ECM2.3

The conscience and consciousness of the stakeholder?

Like all companies, Boots, a major retailing and pharmaceutical group in the UK, has to answer to its shareholders. It has also to answer to its stakeholders. On 22 July 1993 during its annual meeting, at the QE2 conference centre in London, the chairman of the company was challenged by animal rights protesters over the alleged use of animals in the testing of Nurofen and of Manoplax. Eventually police and security personnel were called in to restore calm and several people were removed from the meeting.

D. Generic Strategies for Dealing with Stakeholders

Freeman[4] developed a set of generic strategies for dealing with stakeholders which are valid regardless of which industry is involved. The potential co-operation (the extent to which the stakeholder helps us to achieve our objectives) and the competitive threat (the extent to which stakeholders prevent us from achieving our goals) for each stakeholder are determined and plotted on a chart (see figure ECM2.2).

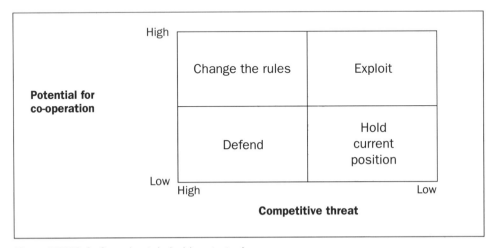

Figure ECM2.2 Generic stakeholder strategies.

Source: Adapted from Freeman, 1984.

Once the stakeholders are plotted on the chart it will be possible to decide how to deal with them. For example, according to this view:

■ Stakeholders with high co-operative potential and low competitive threat indicate the need for the adoption of an offensive strategy to get these stakeholders to co-operate.

■ Stakeholders with high competitive threat and low co-operative potential indicate the need for the adoption of a defensive strategy to prevent the threat that they pose to us.

■ Stakeholders with high co-operative potential and high competitive threat indicate the need to adopt a strategy to change or influence the rules which govern the stakeholder interactions.

■ Stakeholders with both low co-operative potential and low competitive threat indicate the need for the firm to continue with the current strategy.

There are a number of drawbacks to the stakeholder concept:

■ Openness may lead to problems due to difficult issues being brought to the surface. It also highlights the knowledge or ignorance of the managers.

■ Both management and employees must be involved and the knowledge base may not be present in these groups.

■ Paralysis by analysis may occur. This involves time, effort and costs. One must take action – hopefully, action which has been thought through, of course.

Please tackle Activity ECM2.4.

ACTIVITY ECM2.4

STAKEHOLDERS III

Activity code
- ✓ Self-development
- ✓ Teamwork
- ☐ Communications
- ☐ Numeracy/IT
- ✓ Decisions

Task

1 Assess the stakeholders of 'your' organization for potential co-operation and competitive threats.

2 Describe a strategy for dealing with them.

It is important to sense changes in both the stakeholders and the climate in order to flag the need for changes in strategy. This can be done by identifying opportunities and threats. There is evidence to show that organizations good at sensing the environment are better performers. However, simply being able to analyse the environment is not sufficient: organizations also have to be able to respond to change. This will depend on the flexibility, quality and culture of management and the structure of the organization.

Since managers tend to overemphasize the strengths and opportunities and neglect the weaknesses and threats of their businesses, a vulnerability analysis was suggested by Hurd.[5] This is explained in Box ECM2.4, and provides a risk-averse approach which you may wish to consider.

BOX ECM2.4

Risk aversion

A **vulnerability analysis** was suggested by Hurd[1] in order to answer the following question:

> Which supporting elements (underpinnings), if taken away, might seriously damage or even destroy the organization?

Examples of such underpinnings include:

- customer needs and wants
- resources and assets
- cost position relative to competition
- customer base
- technology
- special skills, systems, etc.
- corporate identity
- barriers to competition
- social values
- sanctions, supports and incentives
- goodwill
- complementary products.

Source:

1 Adapted from Hurd, D.A., 'Vulnerability analysis in business planning', *SRI International Research, Report No. 593* (1977).

E. The Competitive Environment

There are several concepts which must be understood in order to make a useful assessment of the competitive environment. These are the customer, product, market and the industry. They will be outlined in the next few pages, but first, consider Box ECM2.5.

The customer

To achieve an organization's goals, it is important for managers to consider their customers together with their needs. One of the beliefs of Peters and Waterman[6] was the necessity for getting close to your customers – supplying their needs for high-quality products and services at a price they can afford.

To manage an organization successfully one needs information, and the most important information is on what the customer wants. Therefore, in the same way as an environmental monitoring system was suggested earlier, so we need a customer monitoring system. A system needs to be set

---

BOX ECM2.5

How competitive is the competitive environment?

The dispute between Virgin Atlantic and British Airways may stretch the limits of fair competition, and it raised ethical considerations on how we conduct our business.

Virgin claimed that British Airways sought details of Virgin's passenger lists and details on its carrying/load factors. Special computing equipment gave access to this information. Commercially sensitive information was seemingly passed to BA management.

Writs and legal action ensued and the whole matter became somewhat unsavoury, involving the senior managers of British Airways, lawyers, and questions in the House of Commons.

---

up to find out who the customers are or will be and what they want. It must be oriented towards the future and the concept of the customer defined broadly.

Taking the definition to the extreme, each person can be a 'customer' of every other person inside the organization, as well as the customers outside it. From this viewpoint, customers are not only buyers of products but also recipients of services provided by each person in the organization free of charge. Each recipient has a need for high-quality service, so the problem for managers is how to develop a quality culture in the organization. Total quality management (TQM) and 'getting it right first time' are just two popular managerial themes of the 1990s. However, in this book we shall concentrate on the actual or potential buyers of the organization's products/services.

There are also two primary demand factors, demographic and geographic, which affect the market for goods and services for different industries.

Demographic factors include changes in the population, including areas such as age and income distribution. Such changes can provide threats or opportunities to an organization and have to be taken into consideration.

Geographic factors must also be considered, since new locations for expansion or relocation are often required. The need for such changes may be due to customer demand or operating costs.

The product

In order to satisfy customer needs we need some products. **Products** are concepts, objects, places, personalities, organizations and services which can be offered for sale. Organizations may have many different products.

The **product concept** is based on:

■ providing a core benefit or service;

■ providing a formal product in terms of styling, features, brand name, packaging and quality;

■ augmentation, which includes installation, service, guarantees and delivery.

The **product mix** is the full list of products offered by an organization and can vary from a single product to multi-lines with multi-products. The product mix has breadth in terms of the number of product lines and depth in the assortment of colours, models and sizes offered on each. For example, Ford sell lines of cars, vans and trucks and within each line are several models, sizes, colours, etc., which are needed or desired by the customers. Managers must understand the contribution of each line and product to the organization's costs and profits. This is important not only for management control, but also for monitoring the product life cycle from development through growth and maturity to decline.

Products, like people, go through a life cycle, since they grow in sales, then decline and are eventually replaced. The period from birth to death is the life cycle. The **product life cycle** reflects product demand as the product moves from introduction through saturation to obsolescence.

The life cycle can be considered to involve four stages: introduction, growth, maturity and decline. Figures in textbooks suggest that these stages are of equal length when in fact they last for different periods of time.

These variations in stages also vary from product to product, and not all products go through all the stages. The slope of the curve of the product's sales graph indicates the speed or rates of demand. A steep upward slope indicates high demand with short introductory or maturity periods. In the same way, demand can decline slowly or quickly.

In general, the **introduction** stage consists of creating awareness and acceptance for the product. Investment continues into the **growth** stage, which shows increasing profits, which in turn attract competitors. During **maturity**, competition reaches its peak. A **decline** in sales and profits follows until the product is withdrawn. However, it may not be until the decline stage that there is maximum recovery of investment.

Each of these stages has implications for managers, since the competitors' distribution, pricing, products and profit margins change as the product moves from one stage to another.

The products of every organization will eventually become obsolete, and as the product ages its profit declines. If ageing products are not changed or replaced, the organization's sales volume and profits will decline. The decline in sales occurs because:

■ the need for the product disappears;

■ a better or cheaper product appears;

■ customers become tired of the product.

Therefore, new products are essential for an organization to survive, let alone grow and make profits.

When a market is growing, a firm can grow simply by keeping up with the demand from the market. It is a very different situation when markets are mature and demand has flattened. In this case growth can only be achieved by taking market share from competitors.

The market

Kotler[7] defines a market as 'the set of individuals or organizations who are actual or potential buyers of a product or service'. He suggests making use of four categories of market:

1 consumer markets – people buying for personal use;
2 producer markets – manufacturers buying materials or parts for their own use;
3 resale markets – people buying for the purpose of reselling;
4 government markets – those buying for government purposes.

He also suggests segmenting those markets into sets of customers with distinct needs. Segments could be based on attitudes, buying practices, locations, needs, resources, size, etc.

Once the segments have been identified, different strategies could be followed:

■ an undifferentiated approach – a single marketing mix for the broadest market;
■ a marketing mix focused on a narrow segment;
■ different mixes for different segments of the market.

The choice would depend on:

■ the characteristics of the products/services
■ the competition
■ the organization's resources
■ the needs of the customers.

The term **marketing mix** is used to describe the **four Ps** – the **p**roduct, its **p**rice, the distribution system (**p**lace) and **p**romotion. The marketing mix is influenced and supported by the organization's internal resources but limited by the environment.

The four Ps are interrelated in that decisions in one area usually affect other areas. Since each of the four Ps contains many variables, it is up to management to select the combination that adapts to the environment, satisfies the market and meets the organization's goals.

The marketing mix is important to managers because it stresses the integrated nature of the four Ps. The mix for any product is a combination of factors which together induce a customer to buy. At the same time, both the product and the buying behaviour of the consumer influence the choice of marketing mix.

F. Market and Product Assessment

Once we have understood the basic concepts of marketing we can focus on methods which will help managers assess their products and markets. An analysis of the market(s), product line(s), product(s), life cycles and the marketing mix should identify the gaps to be filled and improvements to be made. Gaps in the product line or distribution chain, for instance, could lead to management decisions to fill them.

Other factors which need to be examined are the relationships of marketing with the other functional areas in the organization, such as research and development, production and finance. Can these be developed to produce a competitive edge?

Managers can make a product/market assessment by identifying where each of the organization's products stand in its market. Rowe et al.[8] explain **growth vector analysis,** which examines the product, the market and the alternative directions for growth. A new product in an existing market requires a different approach from an existing product in a new market.

As can be seen in figure ECM2.3, a chart can be used to identify the current position. Present products should be listed with their market share, sales, profits, growth, position in life cycle, pricing policies, etc., on a separate chart, and some assessment made. The products can then be listed in block A on the chart, and possible alternatives can be developed. This type of chart is a tool and can be developed in any way you find useful.

	Present products	Improved products	New products
Existing market	A	Variations, imitations	Extend product line
Expanded market	Promote aggressively	Segment market, differentiate products	Diversify vertically
New market	Develop market	Extend market	Diversify, conglomerate

Market options (vertical axis) · **Product alternatives** (horizontal axis)

Figure ECM2.3 Position of each of an organization's products and possible product/market options.

Source: Rowe, A.J., Mason, R.O., Dickel, K.E. and Snyder, N.H., *Strategic Management: a methodological approach* (Addison-Wesley, Reading, MA, 1990).

Please tackle Activity ECM2.5. Box ECM2.6 provides a context of the debate concerning increasing globalization of the marketplace.

ACTIVITY ECM2.5

A MARKETING ASSESSMENT

Activity code
☑ Self-development
☑ Teamwork
☑ Communications
☐ Numeracy/IT
☑ Decisions

Task

Write a report on 'your' work organization or college concerning its customers, products and markets.

BOX ECM2.6

Globalization of the marketplace

To Levitt, globalization of markets is inevitable.[1] Stimulated by technological advance, cheaper products reach the masses across frontiers, transported and communicated by ever greater and faster changes in technology. The global company offers 'high quality, more or less standardized products at optimally low prices, thereby achieving for itself vastly expanded markets and profits. Companies that do not adapt to the new global realities will become victims of those that do.'

Hirst thinks otherwise.[2] He notes four premises behind the globalization theme:

1 Domestic governmental and corporate policies could be subsumed by world markets.
2 The main proponents would be transnational corporations.
3 The power of organized labour would go into even greater decline.
4 Camps would exist of countries which accepted or rejected globalization trends.

We debate the whole issue of globalization at length elsewhere in the series.[3]

Sources:

1 Levitt, T., 'The globalization of markets', *Harvard Business Review*, May/June (1983).
2 Hirst, P., 'Globalisation is fashionable but is it a myth?', *Guardian*, 22 March (1993).
3 Anderson, A.H., Dobson, T. and Patterson, J., *Effective International Marketing* (Blackwell Publishers, Oxford, forthcoming).

University
of Ulster
LIBRARY

G. Industry and the Competitive Environment

So far in this unit we have considered the needs of the customer and the marketplace in which the organization operates. The organization operates not in isolation, however, but in a dynamic competitive environment. A manager has to develop a competitive edge for his or her organization and defend it over time. Therefore, this part of the unit will be devoted to understanding the industry and the competitive environment in which the organization operates.

The difference between an industry and a market is easily understood if you take the car industry as an example. This is made up of several manufacturers which serve several markets – luxury, small-car, off-road, small-van and truck. Some organizations compete on an industry basis while others compete only within the market. For example, Ford competes in the motor-vehicle industry while Land Rover competes in the off-road market. Essentially, an industry is a group of organizations whose products compete for the same buyers.

The analysis of an industry and its competitive environment is a way of ensuring that important features of the organization's environment are not overlooked. Clues to the future are to be found in this work, which should be done periodically in order to detect gradual changes in the industry.

Industries vary in their economic characteristics and competitive environment to such an extent that a well-managed organization can find it difficult to survive in one industry while a poorly managed organization in another industry can make large profits.

In order to try to make some sense of this dichotomy, we shall outline an approach to **industry and competitive analysis** which will help you to build up an understanding of your industry and its competitive environment. This will enable you to make decisions about both the long-term and the short-term attractiveness of the industry.

One method of examining the opposition is to conduct an exercise on competitor profiling (see Box ECM2.7). Activity ECM2.6 should be tackled before examining an alternative approach to industry and competitive environments.

BOX ECM2.7

Competitor profiling

Industry changes will impact on your competitors as well. Part of enterprise management's view of change is to examine these possible changes in the context of the competition and how they all react. This may be a survival approach, as a minimum position, or it may give you the edge over rivals. Of course, if the overall industry or product is in decline (relative or absolute) this competitor analysis may not be the answer, for the scan would have to go further into products and the industry base as well as into the actual or perceived needs of customers.

We can usefully profile our competitors as follows.

Policy

Is there an overall strategy? Is it planned or *ad hoc*? How broad/narrow is that strategy? Are different policies being adopted across the product range, segments, etc.? What are they trying to do – survive, grow, go for market share, etc.?

Organization, personnel and operations

Do other organizations anticipate or react to changes better than you? If so, why? Do they have blind spots? What internal strengths or weaknesses can be seen? Do they have core strengths or weaknesses in the following: functional expertise, skilled staff, research and development (R & D), innovation, *esprit de corps*, reward strategies, efficient operations, an organization structure geared to change, etc.?

Enterprise

What are their track records like? Do they respond to novel challenges? How do they or would they react to, say, a price war? Is there 'weaker' opposition that could be tackled first?

Marketing

- **Product** – a portfolio analysis including approximate contribution by segment should be tackled. Innovation and launch success should be studied. A matrix on the portfolio of each competitor can be attempted to identify their current approach to competition.[1]
- **Place** – distribution outlets and physical distribution can be studied. Channel strategies need to be equated to the product portfolio.
- **Promotion/communications** – the sales team should be examined via your own team. Advertising, its type and its image need to be analysed by competitor. Any other 'contribution', from public relations (PR) to special offers, etc., needs to be analysed.
- **Price** – this is important in most marketplaces. You need to have their price ranges across the product portfolio, with any evidence of discounting, etc. The make-up of or rationale behind the pricing structure needs to be analysed.

Finance

You may have access to their accounts, etc., but these figures may be too global. Best guesses or estimates need to be made on product expenditure, market expenditure, cash flows, etc. Track records in R & D, or any press releases or articles on innovations, should be monitored to give a 'feel' for R & D expenditure. Ultimately the financial domain will dominate, and whether companies attack, hold or defend may come back to their financial strengths or weaknesses.

Source:

1 See Anderson, A.H. and Barker, D., *Effective Business Policy* (Blackwell Publishers, Oxford, 1994), pp. 223–30.

ACTIVITY ECM2.6

COMPETITION I

Activity code
- ✓ Self-development
- ✓ Teamwork
- ✓ Communications
- ☐ Numeracy/IT
- ✓ Decisions

Task

Write a report on 'your' work organization or college covering the 'industry' in which it operates and on its competitive environment.
The report should include:
- factors which make the industry attractive, with reasons;
- factors which make the industry unattractive, with reasons;
- special issues or problems;
- profit outlook.

Thompson and Strickland[9] suggest an alternative method for analysing an industry and its competitive environment:

- Identify the dominant economic characteristics of the industry.
- Identify and assess the driving forces.
- Evaluate the strength of the competitive forces.
- Assess the competitive positions of the competitors in the industry.
- Predict which competitor will be likely to make what competitive moves next.
- Identify the key success factors for the industry.
- Draw conclusions about the attractiveness of the industry both short-term and long-term.

This approach is explained in great detail in *Effective Business Policy* in this series, so we will summarize it here.

Dominant economic characteristics

The first task is to identify the dominant economic characteristics of the industry. These features could range from market size to industry profitability. Please tackle Activity ECM2.7.

ACTIVITY ECM2.7

INDUSTRY: ECONOMIC FEATURES

Activity code
- ✓ Self-development
- ☐ Teamwork
- ☐ Communications
- ☐ Numeracy/IT
- ✓ Decisions

Task

1 Outline the main economic characteristics impacting on 'your' work organization or college (for example, scope of competitive rivalry).
2 Is any feature more of a priority than others? Please give details.

Industry driving forces

The economic characteristics identified earlier are a snapshot of the present time, but they do not tell managers about the forces which have formed the industry as it is and which will shape its future. Managers must

ACTIVITY ECM2.8

INDUSTRY DRIVING FORCES

Activity code
- ✓ Self-development
- ✓ Teamwork
- ☐ Communications
- ☐ Numeracy/IT
- ✓ Decisions

Task

1 What do you (or your group) see as the main driving forces of **any** industry?
2 What do you feel are the key driving forces affecting 'your' industrial or educational sector?

try to identify the key driving forces and the impact they will have on the industry in the future.

Now complete Activity ECM2.8 to consolidate these concepts.

The strength of competitive forces

Porter's **five forces model**[10] is a very useful concept for identifying the key competitive forces in an industry (see figure ECM2.4).

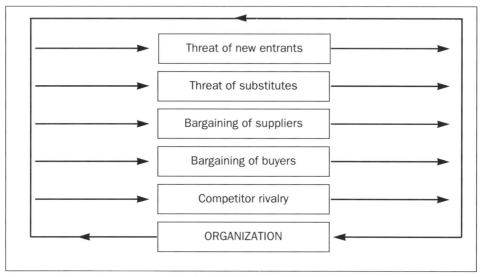

Figure ECM2.4 The five competitive forces.

Source: Adapted from Porter, M.E., *Competitive Strategy: techniques for analyzing industries and competitors* (Free Press, New York, 1980).

By understanding the five competitive forces a manager should be able to:

■ build a sustainable competitive advantage;
■ out-manoeuvre rivals;
■ defend against competitive forces;
■ strengthen the organization's market position.

Please tackle Activity ECM2.9.

The competitive positions of competitors

We looked at this under a different perspective earlier (see Box ECM2.7). It would be useful to consolidate our position to date by tackling Activity ECM2.10.

ACTIVITY ECM2.9

RIVALRY

Activity code
- ☑ Self-development
- ☑ Teamwork
- ☑ Communications
- ☐ Numeracy/IT
- ☑ Decisions

Rivalry among existing firms

Porter[1] likens this to jockeying for position, using tactics such as advertising, better distribution, guarantees, quality or services, new products or features, prices, promotions, etc. The weapons change over time as organizations attack and defend themselves.

Task

Outline potential scenarios or conditions where rivalry between existing firms will be intense.

Source:

1 Porter, M.E., *Competitive Strategy: techniques for analyzing industries and competitors* (Free Press, New York, 1980).

ACTIVITY ECM2.10

COMPETITION II

Activity code
- ☑ Self-development
- ☑ Teamwork
- ☐ Communications
- ☐ Numeracy/IT
- ☑ Decisions

Task

What are the competitive characteristics that differentiate firms in:
(a) any industry?   (b) 'your' industry?

Predicting competitors' moves

Once you have recorded all your competitors you will be able to find out who are your closest rivals. It will be necessary to keep an eye on these and try to predict how they will compete in the future. It is also necessary to predict who will be your major competitors in the future, since some current competitors will lose ground while small firms may be poised to make a major attack on the market with a new product, for instance. So we need to ask ourselves the following questions:

■ Which firms are in favourable positions, and why?

■ Which firms are in unfavourable positions, and why?

Key success factors

These determine the financial and competitive success in the industry. Firms can win competitive advantage in an industry by concentrating on one or two key success factors. There are many types of these.

Please tackle Activity ECM2.11.

ACTIVITY ECM2.11

SUCCESS FACTORS

Activity code

✓ Self-development

✓ Teamwork

✓ Communications

✓ Numeracy/IT

✓ Decisions

Task

By group or individual initiative, brainstorm likely success factors in gaining competitive advantage.

Industry prospects and overall attractiveness

It is now time to review all the information you have collected about the industry. What conclusions can you make about its long-term and short-term attractiveness? An attractive industry encourages the development of an aggressive and expansionist approach, while an unattractive industry encourages a protective approach. Weak firms may have to consider leaving the industry or merging with a rival.

Please tackle Activity ECM2.12. Box ECM2.8 gives an even wider perspective on industrial competitiveness.

ACTIVITY ECM2.12

ATTRACTIVENESS

Activity code

- ✓ Self-development
- ✓ Teamwork
- ✓ Communications
- ✓ Numeracy/IT
- ✓ Decisions

Task

By group or individual initiative, determine what types of factor should be taken into account in considering the attractiveness of an industry.

BOX ECM2.8

National competitiveness

Perhaps we should consider not only industry competitiveness, but national competitiveness. The UK is still well behind its international competitors.[1] UK problems, according to the Department of Trade and Industry, include:

- lower productivity levels (by some 25 per cent) than its rivals;
- a poor skills base, caused presumably by inadequate training;
- poor management – as Dr Dobbie of the Competitiveness Unit said, British industry 'has a long tail' of poor management and 'performance at the tail needs to be improved significantly'.

Source:

1 Beavis, S., 'Britain faces a daunting task to match the competition', *Guardian*, 15 July (1993).

Thus far we have examined the external environments confronting work organizations. The stakeholder concept is seen as very important. As Garrison tells us, 'the increasing influence and power of those outside the competitive marketplace, but who are still vitally concerned with a firm's activities, represent a major power challenge to management'.[11]

The competitive marketplace is still critical, of course, and we spent considerable time in this area. We then turned to specific market and product assessment and widened the discussion further by taking an interactive approach to the industry and competitive environments.

By looking at the external environments we have been conscious both of change and its manifestations from outside the organization, and of the potential (or indeed lack of potential) for enterprise in that external environment.

In the next unit, we look inwards to the organization. The **capability of changing** and the **capacity for enterprise** within the organization are the two themes of this unit.

Notes

1 Levitt, T., 'The globalisation of markets', *Harvard Business Review*, May/June (1983).

2 Anderson, A.H., and Barker, D., *Effective Business Policy* (Blackwell Publishers, Oxford, 1994).

3 Rowe, A.J., Mason, R.O., Dickel, K.E. and Snyder, N.H., *Strategic Management: a methodological approach* (Addison-Wesley, Reading, MA, 1990).

4 Freeman, R.E., *Strategic Management: a stakeholder approach* (Pitman, London, 1984).

5 Hurd, D.A., 'Vulnerability analysis in business planning', *SRI International Research*, Report No. 593 (1977).

6 Peters, T.J., and Waterman, R.H., *In Search of Excellence* (Harper and Row, New York, 1982).

7 Kotler, P., *Marketing Management* (Prentice Hall, New York, 1980).

8 Rowe et al., *Strategic Management*.

9 Thompson, A.A., and Strickland, A.J., *Strategic Management: Concepts and Cases* (Irwin, Homewood, IL, 1992).

10 Porter, M.E., *Competitive Strategy: techniques for analyzing industries and competitors* (Free Press, New York, 1980).

11 Garrison, T., 'Interdisciplinary management rounds', reported in the third round of 'Stakeholder Management', *Henley Newslink*, summer (1994).

ECM Unit Three

The Business Environment

Learning Objectives

After studying this unit you should be able to:
- analyse an organization from a functional viewpoint;
- describe the value chain for an organization and the resources required to support it;
- describe the Seven S Framework for any enterprise;
- describe an organization in terms of the tasks, people and functions involved;
- estimate the responsiveness of an organization;
- understand the key concepts for designing an organization structure;
- understand how decisions are made;
- understand the importance of the international stakeholders for change and enterprise;
- apply the generic skills.

Contents

A. Overview

B. A Functional Perspective

C. The Value Chain Perspective

▶ Resources and the value chain

▶ Evaluating the value chain

D. The Seven S Framework and the TPF Perspective

E. Prerequisite: Responsiveness

F. Prerequisite: An Organic Structure

▶ The technology

G. Prerequisite: Proactive Decision Making

H. Prerequisite: Acceptance of Change and Enterprise by Internal Stakeholders

ECM Unit Three

> ❝ In institutions – including religious institutions – when people talk about unity, they're talking about keeping quiet. It is clear from the Bible that discipleship involves disturbance, being uprooted from what you know.❞
>
> *Dr David Jenkins, then Bishop of Durham*[1]

A. Overview

Clearly the external environments make for change. The internal organizational environment can also make for change, with different management, new styles, products, technologies, methods and practices, etc., all possibilities. Enterprise certainly comes from within the organization, with its ability to exploit external opportunities. Indeed the flexibility, creativity and adaptability of the internal organization, alongside a spirit of enterprise, may be the key themes in managing these changing external environments.

So an internal organizational analysis will demonstrate the change capability and the capacity for enterprise within the organization.

We approach this analysis from various perspectives:

- a purely functional viewpoint
- the value chain analysis
- the Seven S Framework
- a managerial approach of task, people and function (TPF).

We feel that the approaches have their own distinct value for our dual purposes of analysing the capacity for enterprise and the capability of change.

We suggest also the need for some prerequisites – irrespective of the perspective being applied – to facilitate our twin themes of change and enterprise. These prerequisites are:

- responsiveness
- an organic structure
- proactive decision making
- acceptance of change and enterprise by internal stakeholders.

First we look at the four perspectives, then we examine the proposed prerequisites. In the next unit we fuse together concepts of change and enterprise which we have covered to date.

B. A Functional Perspective

Ansoff and McDonnell look at a functional perspective from the vantage point of capability.[2] In our terms this equates to the capacity for enterprise rather than to that for change *per se*, but we can broaden out this analysis to encompass change.

These functions are seen by Ansoff and McDonnell as finance, human resources, marketing, production/operations, and research and development, together with management 'knowhow'.[3] The building blocks of each function are similar in that they use equipment, facilities, knowhow, shared knowledge, skills and technology.

Certain common properties exist in each function as well. These include:

■ a task subdivision

■ related tasks and non-related tasks

■ culture

■ power structure.

Highly subdivided tasks may give efficiency but they also produce rigidity, which may inhibit change. Loosely defined tasks may be more inefficient but more creative, with implications for enterprise.

Partitioned tasks may give greater stability while coupled tasks may produce greater flexibility, with implications for coping with change if not for enterprise.

The predominant 'personality' or culture of the organization can be geared towards efficiency at the expense of flexibility and vice versa. It can have a climate of enterprise or may not have such a personality.

Autocratic power structures within and amongst functions can lead to stability and efficiency; a shared power structure may facilitate change and enterprise at the expense of efficiency.

Please refer to Box ECM3.1. Then, using the same functional list, tackle Activity ECM3.1.

BOX ECM3.1

Functional analysis and change

As we have seen, functional analysis can give us an insight into the distinctive competence of an organization. These strengths can either be linked to external opportunity and/or give some competitive edge over rivals. Either way, both opportunity and edge can stimulate enterprise.

Some form of audit or investigation of these functional areas can therefore be used for an enterprise analysis. The audit can also be used for analysing the propensity for or the possibility of change within the organization. We shall develop this idea below. Please refer to the checklist shown here, which illustrates some possible indicators of change and their implications for the organization.

Operations and buying

Are the costs monitored?	Easily remedied.
Are the levels of R & D and basic research at the optimum levels?	If not, capital injection and new staffing or equipment can alter things.
The technology being used may not meet current demand, etc.	Capital injection may be the answer and technological forecasting could be used.
Issues of scheduling, controlling, engineering, transport and quality come over as difficulties.	This could mean layout or machine problems, but capital injection and people seem to be the possible change agents.

Finance and legal

Is the overall plan related to the corporate plan?	Easily altered.
Investment policy or risk analysis policies need to be established.	Again, this can change through investment analysis quite easily and reasonably 'objectively'.
Capital budgets and larger-term projects must be analysed and scrutinized.	This is a willingness to spend (assuming the money is there) based on objective analysis, so change is possible.
Budgets must reflect an action orientation.	These can become ossified. Change may be more difficult owing to vested interests.
Financial analysis and past or current records can give keen insights into the need for change.	Ongoing monitoring of ratios, for example, can illustrate potential difficulties and the need for change. This is a critical area of control and change.
Too much stock or too many lines is/are being carried.	Easily remedied by a change to a just-in-time (JIT) type of system, for example.

Stock interruption is a possible problem.	The existence and stability of suppliers or the quality, can be changed through long-term deals and contingency planning.
Other financial examples could include cash-flow difficulties, the level of profit margins, and the capital gaining structure.	Ongoing financial monitoring should establish these key indicators.
Do the accounting systems meet business need?	An audit of the systems will be required.
Is the company structure adequate for our purposes?	Consider such issues as the Articles of Association, voting shares and expertise of the directorate. These points can be amended (although the expertise of directors may be a touchy matter).
The degree of family control, if evident, can be problematic.	Unless boardroom coups occur, such family control may be very difficult to break free from.

Marketing

Is research conducted? Does a plan of campaign exist?	Easily remedied.
Is the mix consistent with the plan of campaign? If not, why not?	Change can occur through in-depth analysis and evaluation of the mix.
Does a renewal policy on products operate?	Easily remedied – although costly.

Personnel and organization

Is there a staffing plan consistent with the corporate plan?	Easily remedied.
Consider the records on health and safety, recruitment, selection, training and development policies, and procedures to give a flexible approach to working.	Easily remedied.

Are there 'flexi' agreements with the trade unions?	Perhaps more difficult to change.
Is the skill mix of competency adequate?	Training and development instructions may be required.
Is there a climate of enterprise and change?	An OD internationalist strategy may be required (see Unit One).
Is the work organization clear, with jobs, roles and the organization itself structured to adapt to flexibility, change and opportunity?	More difficult to change.

Management
Is there a strategic plan?
What is the calibre of the
management team?
Is there a climate of enterprise?
Is there a climate of change?
Is there executive leadership and
direction?

} Change is possible in all these instances – but it is not easy.

Conclusion
Changes can occur in each of the functions and they can impact on the enterprise aspect of the organization. In particular, capital is seen as a prerequisite. The marketing philosophy must all be all-pervasive. However, the possibility of and propensity for change is a 'people' matter. We will develop this idea in later units, where people can be seen as the key resource of change management.

ACTIVITY ECM3.1

FUNCTIONAL ENTERPRISE?

Activity code
- ✓ Self-development
- ✓ Teamwork
- ☐ Communications
- ☐ Numeracy/IT
- ✓ Decisions

Task

Refer back to Box ECM3.1. Using the examples of change indicators and possible remedies listed there, extrapolate their implications for enterprise.

The managerial capacity and capability may be tied in with this functional approach. Although managers will tend to have a functional perspective in this type of structure, the organization will need designated general managers. Elsewhere in this series, in *Effective General Management*, it is argued that there is a need for a generalist perspective to permeate all levels of functional management.[4]

General management has the responsibility for the overall performance of the business. The capacity of management is its responsiveness to changes in the environment and can be described by three capability attributes: climate, competence and capacity:

1 **Climate** is the propensity of management to welcome, control or reject change.

2 **Competence** is management's ability to respond.

3 **Capacity** is management's capacity for work.

Equally we could have a climate of enterprise, the competence or the ability to exploit opportunity, and the capacity to do the job, which could also cover enterprise. Clearly the managerial knowhow and approach are instrumental to our aims of enterprise and change.

In *Effective Business Policy*, we spend considerable time conducting an audit of functions to gain competitive edge.[5] This can be altered to take account of our current predisposition.

The results of enterprise can be seen in part through a functionalist perspective. The marketeer, for example, can tell us about the number of new products hitting the marketplace and making their mark. Perhaps the marketeer cannot tell us about missed opportunities – but our competitors can. The people managers can illustrate the climate of enterprise and staff attitudes towards the business opportunities by climate questionnaires and attitudinal structuring through, say, training initiatives.

The operations people can tell us about issues such as quality, which may give our product a competitive edge in the marketplace. The financial specialist can demonstrate profit and loss, while an accountant's perspective may enlighten us as to cost structures and resource issues of fund allocation.[6]

Missed opportunities will be difficult to gauge – by definition – so a competitor analysis using the functional list may help us to discern what key opportunities were exploited and by whom, by function, etc. Box ECM3.2 gives an example of a summary of the financial position of a business which can be used for comparative purposes with competitors, the sector, or on a year-by-year basis for the organization itself.

BOX ECM3.2

Summary of the financial position of the business

The financial position of the business can be summarized on a chart like this:

Ratios	1991	1992	1993	1994	Trend	Standard	Comment
Profitability:							
Gross profit margin							
Net profit margin							
Return on capital employed							
Residual income							
Return on equity							
Liquidity:							
Current ratio							
Quick ratio							
Leverage:							
Total debt/Total assets							
Debt/Equity							
Profit before interest and taxes							
Efficiency:							
Cost of sales/Stock							
Sales/Total assets							
Sales/Working capital							
Debts/Daily sales							
Investment:							
Dividend/EPS							
Price/Earnings ratio							
Earnings per share							
Dividend yield							

The Trend column is completed using arrows ↑ up, → neutral, ↓ down.
The Standard column should indicate the target ratio or industry average.

The Comment column can be used as necessary.

The list can be extended, but choosing standards and tolerance limits is not easy. You can also compare the results with competitors' or industry norms. It is best to identify critical success factors and the measures needed to judge whether these are being achieved.

Rowe et al. suggest another approach to measuring success which involves the identification of four indicators: efficiency, effectiveness, equity and responsiveness:[7]

Efficiency   Doing things right – this is the ratio of output produced to input consumed. For example, one could use:

$$\text{Return on investment} = \frac{\text{Profit}}{\text{Investment}}$$

Effectiveness   Doing things right – this is the degree to which a target has been achieved, such as market share.

Equity   This is the fairness, impartiality or equity with which an organization's stakeholders are treated. It is directly related to social responsibility because of the concern for stakeholders such as shareholders, customers, employees and the community. As we have seen (Unit Two), equity is becoming an increasingly important measure of performance.

Responsiveness This is the extent to which the organization satisfies the demands placed on it, such as average service time per customer.

Now please tackle Activity ECM3.2.

ACTIVITY ECM3.2

STRENGTHS AND WEAKNESSES

Activity code
- ✓ Self-development
- ☐ Teamwork
- ☐ Communications
- ☐ Numeracy/IT
- ✓ Decisions

Task

Using a functional analysis, determine the relative strengths and weaknesses of 'your' work organization or college in terms of enterprise and change.

C. The Value Chain Perspective

We can analyse the organization via its functions to give us some indication of enterprise and of change. Yet the activities of designing, producing, marketing, delivering and supporting products and services are not confined within the business but also include the suppliers, distributors and customers outside it. The extent to which products and services are valued by customers is determined by the way the various activities are performed. Thus these activities form a **value chain**. Successful businesses have a theme running through the value chain, such as low-cost leadership, quality or service.

The concept of value started to be developed in the section on the external environment. Now we are looking at value in a slightly different way – Porter's value chain[8] (see figure ECM3.1). The terms shown in the figure are explored below.

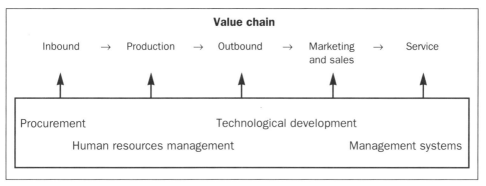

Figure ECM3.1 Porter's value chain concept.

Source: Adapted from Porter, M.E., *Competitive Strategy: techniques for analyzing industries and competitors* (Free Press, New York, 1980).

Every business receives resources, transforms them and sends them as outputs, in terms of products or services, to the customer. This is the value chain, and each of the activities in the chain adds value to the output.

Input, transformation and output consume resources in terms of administration, buildings, equipment, labour, land, management, materials and money. The consumption of resources results in costs to the business.

The value of the output is measured by the total value generated, or:

$$\text{Revenue} = \text{Sale price} \times \text{Number sold}$$

The difference between the total costs and the revenue produces the margin, value-added or operating profit, depending on the term you wish to use.

The efficiency of a business can be measured by the ratio: operating profit/total investment, or return on capital employed (ROCE).

Since what happens in the value chain affects costs and profits, the decisions about each activity in the value chain determine the nature and quality of the output.

A business that seeks to gain advantage by cost leadership tries to reduce resources and the prices it pays for them. A business that seeks to gain advantage by differentiation performs its value-chain activities better than or differently from its competitors. Therefore, identification and improvement of the value-chain activities are probably the best means of gaining a sustainable competitive advantage. They all have to be done well but concentration on one or two can give a competitive advantage.

The generic strategies of cost leadership and differentiation are the basis for business competence or skills. For instance, in order to manage costs effectively it is important to know which cost drivers influence the value chain. Porter identifies the following:[9]

- economies of scale, experience and learning-curve benefits;
- capacity utilization and product control;
- links or liaisons;
- interrelationships and shared activities;
- vertical integration;
- timing of buying and selling;
- standards for procurement and production;
- issues of location;
- institutional factors.

The cost advantage gained is always relative to the competition. Since competitors generally improve, it is usually difficult to catch up once you are behind.

There are opportunities for differentiation in all parts of the value chain, both inside and outside the business. It is important to isolate the key success factors as far as the customers are concerned. It is also important to allocate costs to the value chain and to evaluate whether costs can be saved or additional investment is required to gain additional benefits. Can you add value which the customer will pay for? However, there may be difficulties in allocating costs which have to be addressed in any particular case.

Managers must recognize that the business is primarily there to serve customer needs and not to beat the competition. On the other hand, concentration on the competition may cause management to miss significant changes in the marketplace.

The process of converting inputs to outputs can involve hundreds or even thousands of different activities. Porter classified these as either primary or supporting.[10]

The five **primary activities** which form the value chain are:

1 **Inbound logistics** – the relationships with suppliers, including the activities involved in receiving, storing and internally distributing the inputs, such as

equipment, finance, ideas, materials and people. The activities include stock control, materials handling, vehicle scheduling and warehousing. The activities associated with inbound logistics can be found by identifying the sources of all the incoming resources. Then you ask yourself, 'What activities are necessary to obtain and handle the resources?'

2 **Production** – the activities involved in converting inputs to outputs, such as products and services. Assembling, design, fabrication, machining, maintaining, packaging, process development and testing are included here. You need to identify the activities necessary to convert the inputs to outputs.

3 **Outbound logistics** – the activities necessary for collecting, storing and distributing the output to the customers. Sometimes this may involve getting the customer to the product or service; for example, delivery, materials handling, order processing, scheduling, shipping and warehousing are typical activities. The activities in outbound logistics can be found by identifying where all the outputs are going and what activities are necessary to move the outputs to the customer.

4 **Marketing and sales** – which make customers aware of the product or service, induce them to buy, and facilitate the purchasing process. Advertising, distributing, pricing, promoting, proposing and quoting are typical activities. Marketing and sales activities include all those needed to inform and persuade customers to buy and accept the outputs. Order-taking processes are also important.

5 **Service** – which includes the activities necessary to keep the product or service working effectively for the customer after the sale and delivery. Activities such as consulting, distribution, fine tuning, guarantees, installing, repairing, spare parts and training are involved. Service activities include all the activities needed to maintain customer satisfaction.

To some extent, all businesses perform activities such as these and must be reasonably proficient in them. Superiority in one or two activities can give a competitive advantage. For example, McDonalds is very good at production, marketing and sales. Such superiority may impact on enterprise and change.

The four **support activities** service the primary activities of the value chain and the business itself:

1 **Procurement** is the process of acquiring resources for the primary activities. This is carried out by any employee who acquires resources for the business, except for human resources.

2 **Human resources management** involves all of the activities involved in recruiting, selecting, hiring, training, developing, rewarding and eventually dismissing or laying off personnel. This process affects the overall cost of labour through the salary and wage levels. The overall performance of the business is affected by the level of skill and motivation in it produced by the hiring and training programmes.

3 **Technological development.** All activities have a technology or knowhow associated with the products, processes and resources involved, which include all the design, hardware, software, procedures, and technical knowhow required to convert the inputs to outputs.

4 **Management systems** consist of the functional areas of a business, such as accounting, administration, finance, planning, public relations, quality control and general management. These functions hold the business together and can give a competitive edge if they are working well.

Support activities can be found in several unexpected parts of a business. For example, senior management may not be recruited by the personnel department, and the ordering of new plant may not be done by the purchasing department. Therefore be prepared to look for support activities in all parts of the business.

The support activities described above can provide a business with a competitive edge. For example, certain businesses concentrate on hiring the best managers and others the best technology.

The original objective of this process is to identify or build a core competence or series of core competencies which the business does well compared to its competitors. These represent specialized expertise that competitors do not have and, hopefully, cannot easily obtain.

We can usefully examine this process to highlight potential areas of adaptability or non-adaptability to change and graft on concepts of enterprise. Please tackle Activity ECM3.3.

ACTIVITY ECM3.3

COLLEGE OF EDUCATION: VALUE CHAINS

Activity code
- ☑ Self-development
- ☑ Teamwork
- ☑ Communications
- ☐ Numeracy/IT
- ☑ Decisions

This state-funded college of education has four sites within a 15-mile radius in the south of England. It has approximately the following students: 1,900 full-time, predominantly school-leavers undertaking technician-type courses; 600 day-release from local industry and commerce, undertaking professional and technician-type courses; 2,800 part-time day and evening, who attend an afternoon and two evenings per week from their place of work; and 6,000 purely evening. it has some 220 full-time academic staff, 195 part-time/associate help, and 150 administrative staff, technicians, porters, etc.

In many ways it is a community college rather than an academic centre of excellence. It is involved in adult education in the broadest sense, although increasingly it is becoming more and more vocation-oriented, with a strong presence in business studies, finance and 'languages for business'. The specialisms tend to be reflected in the organizational structure, although older specialisms are still predominant, perhaps at the expense of the newer growth areas of business and languages. There are five faculties:

1 TAD – Technology, Art and Design
2 Communications and Media
3 Social Studies (English, Literature, Sociology and Psychology)
4 Business and Finance
5 Languages.

The 'support' areas include Learning Resources, which is supposed to keep academics abreast of 'best practice'; Student Counselling and Welfare; and an innovation to the college in the last two years, the Marketing Liaison Group. This Marketing Group reflects the educational changes at national level whereby funding from government is being slowly and deliberately reduced per student, while the number (and arguably the quality) of students is increased. The marketing people are there to find additional funding from short courses, language seminars and encouraging overseas students, with or without English as their first language, to boost the coffers, as these individuals pay the full fee without government funding or support. The marketing people would like all students to pay the full fee, and envisage this happening as the state increasingly withdraws its support from this sector. An administrative section co-ordinates all non-academic staff.

There is a senior management team of administrators (with personnel and labour relations support from the Human Resources team). The senior management (six in all) are joined by the five faculty heads to form the directorate. In each faculty, the head is supported by the set leader, who assists with resources, timetabling, staff management and academic development. They hire deputies as well. In addition there is a range of standing committees and sub-committees of the directorate covering academic standards to sexual and racial equality. (See the chart overleaf.)

The students to join the full-time course come primarily from 'lower' colleges and straight from school. The part-timers (day and evening) tend to be at work. The lecturers are employed by the college and they have copyright over ideas and materials. Equipment classrooms and admin. support all emanate from the college authorities. A filing support system exists for student records and placement. On finance, the part-time courses are self-financing while government grants cover the core costs of the full-time students.

The inputs are centred on the college via admin. support for general counselling and careers advice, and from an academic perspective from the lecturers. The library, the bookshop and the computing facility provide the lecturers with learning resources, back-up, their handouts, etc.

The customer is seen as the student and he or she comes to the college for the 'package' to be delivered.

The college prides itself on giving a quality learning experience. There is a tutorial system, a grievance procedure for students, an appeals machinery and a resit facility. The college is strong on equal opportunities.

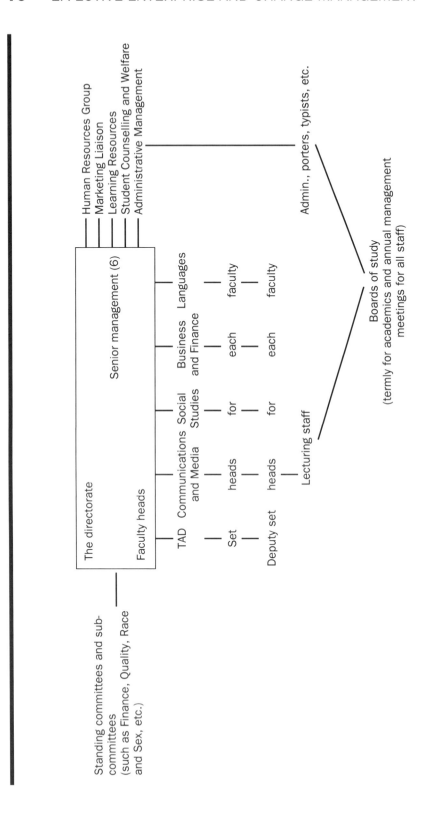

Buying in goods is not a problem as there is an admin. person who co-ordinates this duty. However, new books, videos, film, etc., for classes are not bought in on a regular basis. Interestingly, the computer budget looks almost infinite.

The people policies tend to be bureaucratic. Academics' and admin. staff's pay is low. There seems to be greater job security than in the wider marketplace. Skill and knowledge levels are very high indeed – albeit underutilized. Morale is very low.

The computing section and programmed/interactive learning unit exist as part of the educational technology.

The college is a bureaucracy and it flourishes under a sea of paper with little real accountability, no budgetary control to speak of and inadequate systems. Management pay themselves very well indeed with bonuses per student. These bonuses do not apply to staff.

Tasks

1 Apply the value chain to this case.
2 Outline areas of enterprise which need to be utilized further and note changes that you (or your group) would make.

Resources and the value chain

The resources of a business are distributed among the activities it performs and are part of the value chain. There are four groups of resources:

1 **physical resources** such as buildings, materials, plant and equipment, products, etc. Relevant factors include their age, condition, location, etc.;
2 **human resources** in terms of the number of employees, their adaptability, ages, location, skills, etc.;
3 **financial resources** such as cash flow, investment, sources and uses of money, control, etc.;
4 **intangibles** such as brands, contacts, designs, goodwill, image, logos, patents, reputation, etc.

These resources and activities are organized into systems which produce the products or services for the business. To record the primary activities and resources of a business, we can complete a chart like figure ECM3.2. This can combine the primary activities and the associated resources for each of the support activities. Each support activity indicates the typical resources associated with it. Others can be added as necessary. When completed, these charts should be analysed to identify the key linkages or the linkages which can be developed to provide a competitive advantage.

Support activity, such as procurement

	Inbound logistics	Operations	Outbound logistics	Marketing and sales	Service
Physical resources					
Human resources					
Financial resources					
Intangibles					

Figure ECM3.2 Primary activities and resources required in the support activities of the business

Evaluating the value chain

Once you have identified the primary and support activities and the resources required, you need to identify the key objectives and the measurements required for each of them. This will enable you to determine the strengths and weaknesses of your enterprise. See Box ECM3.3, and then please tackle Activity ECM3.4.

BOX ECM3.3

Key organizational strengths and weaknesse

Here are some key examples:	Measurements	Strength	Weakness
■ inbound logistics			
■ production			
■ outbound logistics			
■ marketing and sales			
■ service			
■ procurement			
■ human resources management			
■ technological development			
■ management systems			
■ physical resources			
■ human resources			
■ financial resources			
■ intangibles.			

ACTIVITY ECM3.4

SOME OBJECTIVES

Activity code

☑ Self-development
☑ Teamwork
☑ Communications
☑ Numeracy/IT
☑ Decisions

Task

From Box ECM3.3, define key objectives and measures of performance for each of the categories in the list. You should focus on the strengths, not the weaknesses.

Once the strengths and weaknesses of the enterprise have been identified, they need to be compared to the opportunities and threats presented by the environment (see Unit Two). This analysis of the value chain will enable you to identify the key competencies for dealing with the threats and exploiting the opportunities. Hence the value chain should be a gauge of enterprise.

It can also highlight what needs to alter to cope with external and indeed internal changes. Please tackle Activity ECM3.5.

ACTIVITY ECM3.5

EVALUATE YOUR VALUE CHAIN

Activity code

☑ Self-development
☐ Teamwork
☐ Communications
☐ Numeracy/IT
☑ Decisions

Task

Evaluate the value chain of 'your' work organization or college or a firm of your choice.

D. The Seven S Framework and the TPF Perspective

The success of an organization is ultimately determined by its ability to design, produce, market and deliver its products or services. Waterman et al.[11] argue that the **Seven S Framework** facilitates this understanding of business effectiveness. In *Effective General Management* in this series we develop this approach to examine the internal business environment of the organization, so we will be brief in this review. See Box ECM3.4 for an overview of the subject.

BOX ECM3.4

The Seven S approach

Cluster	Comment
Strategy	Overall policies used to deal and cope with competitive forces.
Structure	Covers the framework of how the organization allocates its tasks, roles and decision-making apparatus.
Systems	The basis of management intelligence, control and co-ordination in the organization.
Style	The approach to leadership of the management in the organization.
Staff	Employees and their approach, motivation, etc.
Skills	The competence of employees.
Shared values	A normative approach which suggests that a unified belief system (that is, a managerial belief system) should be in place.

Source:
Waterman, R.H., Peters, T.J. and Phillips, J.R., 'Structure is not organisation', *Business Horizons*, June (1980).

So far as our needs are concerned, the Seven S Framework would suggest that:

■ the capacity for change depends on more than one factor;

■ it is a system, so there is a knock-on impact if you change one of these variables;

■ the situation determines the reality and there is no clear start or finish in applying the Seven S formula.

We take this further in the next three units and advocate that the emphasis placed on an aspect of the Seven S Framework is affected by the policy or prevalent situation of relative stability, decline or growth.

Please tackle Activity ECM3.6.

ACTIVITY ECM3.6

THE SEVEN S FRAMEWORK

Activity code

☑ Self-development
☐ Teamwork
☐ Communications
☐ Numeracy/IT
☑ Decisions

Task

From the Seven S analysis, derive from each 'S' the implications for:

1 the capacity for enterprise;
2 the capability of change.

This Seven S Framework is seen here as a useful technique for examining change if not enterprise. Interestingly, Watson[12] studied the way managers use the approach and suggests that they tend towards reliance on strategy, structure and systems, whereas leaders are inclined to make more use of the so-called 'soft' Ss – style, staff, skills and shared values. Watson believes that the Seven S approach to management is the approach used by the leader rather than the manager.

To some extent we develop this leadership concept in Box ECM3.5 on the TPF Perspective.

BOX ECM3.5

The TPF Perspective

The TPF Perspective is an analytical approach to management developed by Anderson.[1] The **T** stands for the task or job in hand; **P** means people; and **F** means the various functions of management. It is argued that management involves a combination of these T, P and F factors. Seniority, the organization, the individual's role perception and other contingent factors will alter the weightings of these three factors, but it is felt that they will still prevail and will be common across all work organizations.

Let us touch upon the three clusters or factors:

1 **Task elements.** These involve 'harder' aspects of management concerned with goal achievement. Control, co-ordination, goal setting, planning and decision making will be involved.

2 **People elements.** These are 'softer' aspects of management involved with the attainment of the task through people. Leading, motivating, teamwork and communication would be involved in this area.

3 **Functional aspects**. These disciplines cross over the task and people elements and we focus on marketing and sales, operations and enterprise, finance and accounting, and personnel management from a specialist's perspective.

The TPF approach will assist you in considering change and enterprise.

Source:

1 Anderson, A.H., Effective General Management (Blackwell Publishers, Oxford, forthcoming).

Inherent in the TPF Perspective is the vision of a generalist manager, for it is argued that all managers have generalist aspects to their job. This organizational vision of management also involves anticipation and responsiveness – both key elements in understanding change and enterprise.

E. Prerequisite: Responsiveness

The organization's capacity to change and to adapt and adopt goes to the root of our subject. Much of the change emanates from outside the organization, so its responsiveness to change may be critical. Of course, a proactive approach to change, with monitoring and environmental scanning mechanisms in place, can only facilitate this awareness of change. There seem to be various types of responsiveness which may serve the different goals of the organization (see figure ECM3.3).

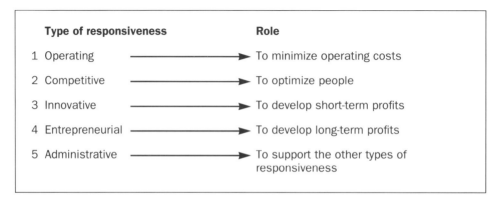

Figure ECM3.3 Responsiveness.

Operating and competitive responsiveness ensure the profitability of the firm's present products in its present markets, whereas innovative and entrepreneurial responsiveness develop the potential for the future profitability of the business. The administrative response must be anticipatory, dynamic, complex and flexible. The use of computers may enable these demands to be met.

Whereas profit centres tend to be responsible for the short-term performance of a business – that is, the operating and competitive responsiveness – the **strategic business unit** (**SBU**) is responsible for both short-term and long-term performance – organization capability.

Mention of the SBU makes it necessary to differentiate it briefly from a similar concept – the **strategic business area** (**SBA**). Please refer to Box ECM3.6. Then tackle Activity ECM3.7.

BOX ECM3.6

SBAs and SBUs

The strategic business area (SBA) is a distinct part of the environment in which the firm does or may wish to do business. It has distinct trends, threats and opportunities.

Most managers view their business environment from the point of view of their current products or services and the ways they can sell them into that environment. However, managers should really think of the business environment as a field of future needs which any competitor can address – the SBA.

An SBA can be described by identifying the:

- need for products or services
- technology to serve the need
- customer type which has the need
- geographical region in which the need will be served.

To be able to compare SBAs we need to know for each one the:

- growth prospects
- profitability prospects
- expected turbulence
- success factors.

To make use of this concept, the first step is to identify one or more SBAs in which your business might be interested. Compare their growth, profitability, turbulence and success factors.

A strategic business unit (SBU) could be responsible for one or more SBAs, so a business could have a portfolio of SBAs. It seems sensible for a business to develop such a portfolio in order to spread risk both at the present time and into the future.

ACTIVITY ECM3.7

ORGANIZATIONAL RESPONSIVENESS

Activity code
☑ Self-development
☐ Teamwork
☐ Communications
☐ Numeracy/IT
☑ Decisions

Task

Using the discussion to date, estimate the responsiveness of 'your' work organization or college, or a firm of your choice.

F. Prerequisite: An Organic Structure

The structure of the organization is there not only to ensure shape and form, but to act as a means of achieving the goals of the organization. Please refer to Box ECM3.7.

BOX ECM3.7

The organization structure

The structure is the skeleton of the organization. It exists to hold the body together and to co-ordinate activity, and acts as a medium for putting policy into effect. Hence the structure has to be geared to both enterprise and change. Often, though, structures become ossified and red tape prevails at the expense of the capacity for change and enterprise.

Elsewhere we examine organizational structures in depth and note the fundamental division between the 'principles approach' and that of contingency.[1] We will not become embroiled in this debate here. Instead we will argue that there is some need for a flexible structure to cope with enterprise and change. Yet even within this flexibility, we need **guidelines** to avoid a dysfunctional, anarchic structure which would hinder the capacities that we wish to pursue.

Some guidelines may include:

Aims	Management and employees should know what the organization is doing or aspiring to do. This must be common knowledge – although the details of the corporate plan will be less commonly known.
Approaches and policies	Management and employees need some policy overview of how their activities dovetail into the policies emanating from the overall aims.
Responsibilities	Cast-iron departments with associated, detailed job specifications must be avoided, but likeminded or related activities, functions or processes need to be linked or grouped together. Bigger rather than smaller jobs should be the order of the day.
Authority	People need to know the parameters of what they can and cannot do. The numbers of levels of authority must be minimized and the 'chain of command', although not long, should be widely known.
Type	There is no ideal type; possibilities range from geographical structures to project teams. The structure must be flexible – whatever its form – and capable of reforming itself as well. It should be more organic than mechanistic, though (see text for more on this).
People	Too often people are appendages to the task. It is the people in the firm that give it its enterprise philosophy and allow it to change, so considerable scope and discretion must be built into any structure.

Source:

1 See Anderson, A.H., *Effective General Management* (Blackwell Publishers, Oxford, forthcoming), and Anderson, A.H., and Kyprianou, A., *Effective Organizational Behaviour* (Blackwell Publishers, Oxford, 1995).

How do we design this organic organization which can facilitate both enterprise and change? The classic work of Burns and Stalker, on about twenty British industrial firms in the 1950s, is a landmark in the study of organization design.[13] They concluded that environmental forces are felt directly by the enterprise and that the structure of an enterprise varies according to the environment. Unstable environments mean rapid changes in competitors, economic conditions, markets, products and technology.

Burns and Stalker discovered that there were two major types of structure which are effective in different environments. Mechanistic (bureaucratic) structures are effective in stable environments and organic (adaptive) structures are effective in unstable environments. These are illustrated in figure ECM3.4.

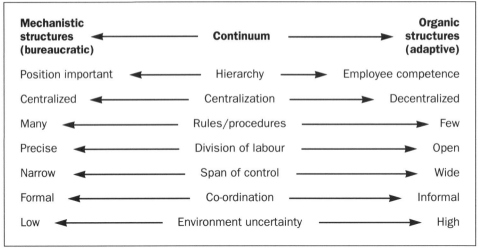

Figure ECM3.4 The continuum between mechanistic and organic structures.

This concept has been developed further in recent years, because environments can be described in terms of their stability and complexity.[14] This is illustrated in figure ECM3.5.

Simple environments have few competitors, one market and little government regulation; for example, a village shop.

Complex environments have strong competition, many customers and suppliers, geographical diversity and high government regulation; for example, a high-street bank.

Stable environments show little or no change over time and any change can generally be predicted; for example, many commodity producers.

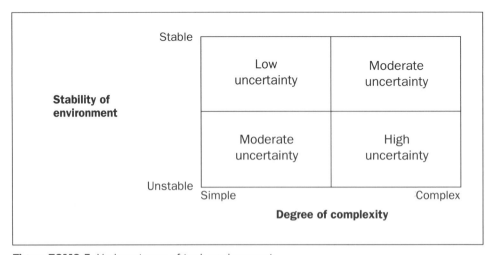

Figure ECM3.5 Various types of task environment.

Source: Hellriegal, D., Slocun, J.W., and Woodman, R.W., *Organisational Behaviour* (West Publishing Co., St Paul, MN, 1989).

Unstable environments show rapid, unpredictable change due to rapid product innovation, changes in demand, market changes, competitors entering and leaving the industry and changes in government regulations; for example, the computer industry.

The technology

'Technology' is normally associated with the nature of the equipment used to complete the tasks of the business. However, in this case 'technology' refers to the science of applying information and knowledge to solving problems, that is, technology as a technique.

Three technological factors influence the number of departments in a business, the delegation of authority and responsibility and the need for a formal integrating mechanism. These are the workflow uncertainty, the task uncertainty, and the task interdependence.

1 **Workflow uncertainty** concerns the degree of knowledge in a department about when inputs can be expected for processing. It is low when a department has little discretion to decide which tasks can be performed when or where.

2 **Task uncertainty** concerns the degree of well-defined knowledge in a department regarding the performance of tasks assigned to it. It is low when members of the department know how to perform the desired tasks and high when members of the department have to use experience, judgement and intuition to solve problems.

3 **Task interdependence** concerns the degree to which decision making and co-operation are necessary to perform a task. It can be classified into three types:

   - **pooled** occurs when each employee or department is not required to interact with others to complete a task – for example, mailing brochures or the sales office of a large business;

   - **sequential** occurs when each employee or department must complete certain tasks before other employees can perform their tasks, as in mass production;

   - **reciprocal** occurs when outputs from one employee or department become inputs for others and vice versa, as can be found in a family or team. This may involve collaboration, communication and group decision making.

The importance of the structure as it relates to technology is illustrated by the classic work of Woodward.[15]

Technology in the service sector:

- focuses the efforts of people with special expertise, such as doctors or teachers, onto the needs of the clients;

- links together people needing a mutually beneficial exchange, such as buyers and sellers;

- passes a client from one point to another for various aspects of the service, as in a self-service restaurant.

The structure of the enterprise must reflect the congruence of the tasks, people, technology and information, or control processes. Further, the organization provides a co-ordinating mechanism for the work effort. See Box ECM3.8.

BOX ECM3.8

The organization as a co-ordinating mechanism

Both change and enterprise need managing and co-ordinating. The organization can provide the means to meet this need. In particular, the division of labour and specific co-ordinating mechanisms can be used.

The division of labour involves role and task specification in an organization. Lawrence and Lorsch show us four types of such division:[1]

- **horizontal** division through similar jobs/tasks;
- **vertical** division through 'tall' and 'flat' structures;
- **personal** division through expertise, ability, specialism, etc.;
- **geographical** division through many locations, etc.

To Hackman and Oldham this rigid division of labour is a constraint on individual and organizational effectiveness.[2] It leads to people being underchallenged, poor or low job satisfaction and commitment, a lack of adaptability and a resistance to change – even when change is a good idea. Their solution lies with a closer marriage between people, their jobs and the redesign of work. Greater autonomy, more feedback, a greater variety of skills and an identifiable and significant task are all advocated in this job redesign.

Whether we accept the traditional approach or the more radical one epitomized by Hackman and Oldham, some organizational integration or co-ordination will still be required. Mintzberg sees five co-ordinating mechanisms:[3]

- **mutual adjustment** or informal communications involving people talking directly to one another. This is very important, as is adapting to the positions of others and getting a 'feel' of how people see your views.
- **direct supervision** or more formalized control, where one individual is in charge of a group. Too many levels of supervision kill any enterprise from below and slow down the reaction time of adaptability to change.
- **standardization of work**. Rules, procedures, work specifications and manuals predominate under this rule-bound bureaucracy. It may be efficient but it is not effective.
- **standardization of output**. The results of work are geared to established specifications, and bonus pay and marginal key results are all linked to output. This may give a high-quality end product, which can only facilitate better customer relations, an area which in turn is linked to enterprise vision.
- **skill standardization**, which can also occur. Again, this may result in a high-quality approach to competencies, but if the pitch is too low it can result in a form of deskilling: we are then back to the job design difficulties identified by Hackman and Oldham, which inhibit change and enterprise.

Sources:

1 Lawrence, P.R. and Lorsch, J.W., 'Differentiation and integration in complex organisations', *Administrative Science Quarterly*, 12 (1967), pp. 1–47.
2 Hackman, J.R., and Oldham, G.R., *Work Redesign* (Addison-Wesley, Reading, MA, 1980).
3 Mintzberg, H., *The Structuring of Work* (Prentice Hall, Englewood Cliffs, NJ, 1980).

Next we can turn to decision making

G. Prerequisite: Proactive Decision Making

Responsiveness, fluid attitudes, organic structures and co-ordinated efforts from within the organization are not sufficient for our purposes. We need to be able to make decisions – often in uncertain situations involving risk, bias, groupthink and no real structure.

It is useful to place decision situations on a continuum from predictable to unpredictable. Three words describe positions on this continuum: certainty, risk and uncertainty.

Under **certainty**, we know what will happen, since there is accurate, measurable reliable information on which to base decisions. In fact, the future is predictable.

When predictability is lower, **risk** exists, since we do not have complete information but we do have an idea of the probability of the result. Probability is the degree of likelihood (for instance, five chances out of ten) that an event will occur.

Under **uncertainty**, very little is known and we are not sure of the probabilities or even the probable results. There are two sources of uncertainty:

1 conditions may be partly or entirely beyond a manager's control;

2 the manager may not be aware of all the information available, or the information may not exist.

Managers in this situation depend on educated guessing, hunches and intuition, which leave a lot of room for error.

Drucker[16] believes that risks should be viewed as limitations on action, and identifies four kinds of risk:

1 the risk one must accept;

2 the risk one can afford to take;

3 the risk one cannot afford to take;

4 the risk one cannot afford not to take.

Simon[17] believes that managers have to cope with:

■ inadequate information about the nature of the problem and its possible solutions;

■ lack of time and/or money to obtain more information;

■ distorted perceptions of the information available;

■ the inability of the memory to retain large amounts of information;

■ the limits of their intelligence to determine the best solution.

These problems cause managers to settle for a decision which will adequately serve their purpose rather than the ideal solution. They **satisfice,** or accept the first satisfactory decision that will serve their purpose, rather than **maximize,** or search to find the optimum decision.

Bazerman[18] cites certain biases which distort decision-making. See Box ECM3.9.

BOX ECM3.9

Bias[1]

Easy recall	Recentness and the vividness of an event can bias judgement.
Insensitivity to prior probability	People tend to overrate the importance of representative information and underrate the importance of basic trends.
Insensitivity to sample size	Statistically, the smaller the sample the more likely it is to stray from the mean.
Misconception of chance	People assume that multiple random events are connected.
Insufficient adjustment	People sometimes arrive at final decisions by adjusting some initial value to suit a specific situation. The initial value may be wrong and this error is therefore continued.
Overconfidence	People do not adjust their level of confidence in their judgement to reflect their actual knowledge about a subject.
The confirmation trap	Often people do not try to discredit their tentative decisions but tend to look at the evidence in their favour.
Hindsight	Once people know the outcome of a decision they may start to believe that they could have predicted it ahead of time. They do not remember how uncertain the situation originally looked, and do recall the evidence as more clear than it actually was.

If you can develop an awareness of such biases, then the quality of your decisions should improve.

Source:
1 Adapted from Bazerman, M.H., *Judgement in Managerial Decision Making* (Wiley, New York, 1988).

To make a decision we need criteria for evaluating courses of action:
- acceptability
- benefits

- costs
- ethical soundness
- timeliness.

Managers can make decisions themselves or involve others. Maier[19] identified two criteria for appraising the effectiveness of a decision: the **quality** of the decision and the **acceptance** of the decision by those who carry it out.

If the decision is based on carefully collected and evaluated facts, then the resulting decision should have high objective quality, especially if it is a technical one. It is an expert or quality decision. However, if people are involved and they have to make it effective, then acceptance of the decision by the people concerned may be important.

Subordinates should be involved in decision making when the benefits in terms of quality, acceptance, morale and development are likely to be greater than the likely costs in terms of time, money or the frustration of those who feel they should not be involved.

The effectiveness of group decisions, however, can be affected by **groupthink**. Janis defines this as 'a deterioration of mental efficiency, reality testing and moral judgement which results from in-group pressures'.[20] In effect a group just drifts along and this may have been evident, for example, in the 'Bay of Pigs' invasion of Cuba.

According to Janis, the symptoms of groupthink are as follows.

- A sense of invulnerability, optimism and risk taking lead to an unquestioned belief in the morality of the group.

- The pressures on the members of the group to conform and reach a consensus means that unpopular or minority ideas may be suppressed. Indeed, members who oppose the group may be stereotyped as evil, weak or stupid.

- The need for a group consensus can result in a rationalization by members to discount warnings, which gives an illusion of unanimity. This leads to self-censorship of any deviation from group norms – apparent consensus.

Kogan and Wallach[21] found there was evidence to show that groups take more risky decisions than individual group members. According to Clark,[22] this is because:

- people inclined to take risks are more influential in group discussions than the more conservative types;

- risk taking is regarded as a desirable cultural characteristic, which is more likely to be expressed in such a social situation as group working.

Shaw, however, cites evidence to suggest that groups produce more and better decisions than individuals.[23] Groups are better at evaluating ideas and those tasks requiring a range of knowledge and expertise.

Rowe et al. have developed a holistic approach to understanding behaviour and performance in organizations[24] (see figure ECM3.6). They believe that when people make decisions in an organization they react to four forces. Any manager who cannot cope with one or more of the forces will ultimately exhibit poor performance, anxiety, conflict, stress, lack of motivation, frustration or withdrawal from the organization.

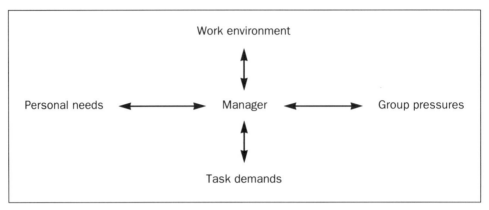

Figure ECM3.6 The Four Force Model.
Source: Rowe, A.J., Mason, R.O., Dickel, K.E. and Snyder, N.H., *Strategic Management: a methodological approach* (Addison-Wesley, Reading, MA, 1990).

The Four Force Model illustrates four different approaches to the study of management. For example, the work environment factors are often explored in economics, business policy and strategy. Psychologists have explored personal needs and group pressures, while industrial psychologists and engineers have tended to concern themselves with the tasks.

Work environment comprises:
- **internal factors** – organization structure, climate (openness, power, support, trust), age of equipment, facilities and manufacturing processes.
- **external factors** – political, economic, social and technical (PEST).

A manager's **situational sensitivity** is the ability to react to and interact with both the internal and external environments. Situational sensitivity is more useful in an open organization, where there is freedom and participation, than in a structured, power-oriented organization that demands compliance and leaves little room for manoeuvre.

Group pressure reflects the manager's interaction with other members of the organization – peers, superiors and subordinates. These interactions influence both performance and commitment. A manager's reaction to a group depends on the type of group, the role and status, and the interpersonal competence. This last is the ability to listen and communicate, deal with pressure to conform, resolve conflict and get on with others.

Task demands are based on the tasks assigned to managers and their abilities to carry them out – skills, technical competence, experience, attitude, willingness to exert effort, satisfaction, and expectations of outcomes and reward.

Personal needs compellingly influence a manager's reaction to environmental, organizational and task demands and needs for affiliation, achievement and power.

Although these four forces have been separated out, they interact and merge with one another, so that, for example, the work environment is involved with task demands.

H. Prerequisite: Acceptance of Change and Enterprise by Internal Stakeholders

Decision making does not just rest with management; the needs and aspirations as well as the views of the other internal stakeholders should be considered for our purposes of change and enterprise. Box ECM3.10 illustrates the important role of the internal stakeholders, while Box ECM3.11 demonstrates a topical approach to spreading the gospel amongst the internal stakeholders through 'empowerment'.

BOX ECM3.10

Internal stakeholders

Internal stakeholders are part of the environment a manager is responsible for. The firm's **employees** are important stakeholders, especially during periods when the workforce is changing. Changes in the birth rate, the influence of ethnic minorities, skill shortages and employee involvement are increasing the stake of the employee in the organization. Employees can also be the sources of new ideas and must be regarded as company assets and be nurtured in order for the organization to prosper.

Shareholders have a stake in the organization in that they expect a return on their investment and also expect it to grow in value. There are different types of shareholder, both private and institutional, each of which makes demands on the organization that have to be reconciled by the manager.

The **boards of directors** have a duty to:

- ensure the continuity of management;
- protect the shareholders' investment;
- ensure management is prudent;
- approve major financial and operational decisions of management;
- represent the organization in society;
- enforce, maintain and revise the corporate charter and by-laws.

The board is a legal entity and a representative of the owners. However, outside representation on the board is becoming more common and can be an effective way of involving major stakeholders with the organization. Boards are also tending to become smaller in order to get more done in the time available, since the environment is becoming more turbulent.

BOX ECM3.11

Empowerment and ownership

Empowerment, a form of individual involvement on the job, seems to be one of the latest fads of human resources management. The cynical would argue that it is merely the knock-on consequence of 'delayering' and 'leaner' organizations; that is, the middle managers are being removed wholesale in a purge from the top. Their administrative duties need to be absorbed, and who better to take this on than the workers, in order to get more scope and responsibility in their work. Greater intrinsic job satisfaction rather than extrinsic financial rewards seems to be the effect of this 'empowerment'.

Now there is nothing wrong in taking responsibility for the job or indeed in building jobs up, but it seems to be a form of 'involvement', not real worker participation.[1] The job may be 'owned' but the organization is not.

From our perspective of enterprise, we do not see Pickard's example[2] of giving out silver badges or team expert badges (*à la* stars at primary school) as making a real contribution to employee participation.

The contribution to enterprise as a whole is debatable, and the idea has the marks of an HRM fad.

Sources:

1 See Anderson, A.H., *Effective Labour Relations* (Blackwell Publishers, Oxford, 1994).

2 Pickard, J., 'The real meaning of empowerment', *Personnel Management*, November (1993).

Empowered or not, the internal stakeholders may be one of the keys to the whole concept of change and enterprise. Other prerequisites have been put forward as well, and these may be as important. The analytical techniques of the Seven S Framework and of the TPF Perspective will be used in the remaining units to develop our views on enterprise in the context of changing scenarios.

Activity ECM3.8 is used to demonstrate how stakeholders react in times of stress. Complete this activity before starting the next unit.

ACTIVITY ECM3.8

THE BLACKBURN LOOM BREAKERS

Activity code
☑ Self-development
☑ Teamwork
☑ Communications
☐ Numeracy/IT
☑ Decisions

As early as 1768 a mob, fearing that they would be put out of work, destroyed twenty spinning machines that the Oswaldtwistle inventor James Hargreaves was building. This did not halt the march of progress, and twenty years later the spinning wheel was obsolete and Samuel Crompton's 'mule' could turn out 400 spindles at a time. Since all that yarn had to be woven into cloth, weaving machines were invented, and Edmund Cartwright built the first power loom in 1784.

The new machines began to produce better-quality fabrics faster and with less labour, so that by the beginning of 1826 trade and commerce were in such a depressed state that businesses were failing daily. The hand-loom weavers were self-employed and were experiencing particular hardship. Over 60 per cent had no work at all. Parliament was being petitioned to repeal the Corn Laws, which restricted the import of cheaper foreign grain.

In the winter of 1826, the *Blackburn Mail* printed a letter from the Secretary of the Weavers' Union Society of Blackburn, addressed to the Home Secretary Robert Peel, in which he said that by operating power looms one boy or girl was able to produce as much work as several hundred hand-loom weavers. This forced the hand-loom weavers to reduce their prices to meet the competition. Reduction had followed reduction until the current wages were 80–90 per cent less than they had been twenty-five years before.

The editorial in the same paper said:

> There is an extent to which the ingenuity of man may be exercised with the benefit to his fellow creatures, but every step beyond it becomes an evil, and we are afraid we must class the invention of the power loom amongst the latter … The invention and use of power looms was not needed, and as they necessarily tend to reduce the demand, and consequently the price of human labour, a large portion of our redundant population were thereby deprived of employment.

The editor of the *Bolton Chronicle* about the same time said: 'At all events something must be done, or the country will be involved in ruin, starvation, revolution and bloodshed.'

By March 1826, only about 2,800 out of about 11,000 cotton operatives in Blackburn had regular employment. The starving hand-loom weavers saw the power looms as the cause of their distress and rose *en masse*, systematically destroying over a thousand of them. Sixty-four men and women were charged with offences relating to the riots, and many were killed and injured in clashes with the army.

Historical sketches like this bring home to us the fact that environmental turbulence is not confined to the end of the twentieth century.

Task

Compare and contrast the introduction of the power loom with the downsizing of industry in western countries during the last few years.

Source:

Martin, C.M., 'The Blackburn loom breakers'. *Lancashire Family History and Heraldry Society*, May/November (1994).

Notes

1 Cited by Watts, J., 'Turbulent priest vows to be silent', *Observer*, 4 July (1993).
2 Ansoff, I.H. and McDonnell, E.J., *Implanting Strategic Management* (Prentice Hall, Englewood Cliffs, NJ, 1990); see also Anderson, A.H., *Effective General Management* (Blackwell Publishers, Oxford, forthcoming).
3 See also Anderson, A.H. and Barker, D., *Effective Business Policy* (Blackwell Publishers, Oxford, 1994).
4 Anderson, *Effective General Management*.
5 Anderson and Barker, *Effective Business Policy*.
6 See Anderson, A.H. and Nix, E., *Effective Accounting Management* (Blackwell Publishers, Oxford, 1995). Also, Anderson, A.H. and Ciechan, R., *Effective Financial Management* (Blackwell Publishers, Oxford, 1995).
7 Rowe, A.J., Mason, R.O., Dickel, K.E. and Snyder, N.H., *Strategic Management: a methodological approach* (Addison-Wesley, Reading, MA, 1990). We could use these criteria to measure not only the success of your own organization but also the track records of others.
8 Porter, M.E., *Competitive Strategy: techniques for analyzing industries and competitors* (Free Press, New York, 1980).
9 Ibid.
10 Ibid.
11 Waterman, R.H., Peters, T.J. and Phillips, J.R., 'Structure is not organisation', *Business Horizons*, June (1980).
12 Watson, C.M., 'Leadership management and the seven keys', *Business Horizons*, March/April (1983), pp. 8–13.
13 Burns, T. and Stalker, G.M., *The Management of Innovation* (Tavistock Publications, London, 1961).
14 Hellriegel, D., Slocum, J.W. and Woodman, R.W., *Organisational Behaviour* (West Publishing Co., St Paul, MN, 1989).
15 Woodward, J., *Industrial Organisation: theory and practice* (Oxford University Press, Oxford, 1965).
16 Drucker, P.F., *Managing for Results* (Heinemann, London, 1989).
17 Simon, H.A., *Models of Man: social and rational* (Wiley, New York, 1957).
18 Bazerman, M.H., *Judgement in Managerial Decision Making* (Wiley, New York, 1988).

19 Maier, N.R.F., *Problem Solving Discussions and Conferences: leadership, methods and skills* (McGraw-Hill, New York, 1963).

20 Janis, I. *Group Think: psychological studies of policy decisions* (Houghton Mifflin, Boston, 1982).

21 Kogan, N., and Wallach, M.A., 'Risk taking is a function of the situation, the person and the group' in *New Directions in Psychology*, ed. T.M. Newcombe (Holt, Rinehart and Winston, New York, 1967).

22 Clark, R.O., 'Group-induced shift towards risk: a critical approach', *Psychological Bulletin*, 76 (1971), pp. 251–70.

23 Shaw, M.E., *Group Dynamics* (McGraw-Hill, New York, 1976).

24 Rowe, et al., *Strategic Management*.

ECM Unit Four

Steady State

Learning Objectives

After completing this unit you should be able to:
- describe your organization in terms of the products/services it provides, the markets its serves and the functions it performs;
- analyse your organization to determine whether it is in the steady state, recovery or growth situation;
- decide whether your organization should remain in a steady state, recover or grow;
- develop the steady state of your organization;
- link change and enterprise through the creation of a vision for your organization;
- determine the operational objectives for your vision;
- make plans to achieve the objectives;
- apply the generic skills.

Contents

A. Overview

B. Generic Strategies

▶ Products/services, markets and functions

▶ Variations of the generic strategies

▶ Choosing your generic strategy

C. Steady State

▶ Introduction

▶ The steady state scenario

▶ An analysis of the steady state: the Seven S Framework

D. Change and Enterprise

▶ The vision

▶ Performance objectives and milestones

▶ Competitive advantage: seeking and maintaining

E. Developing the Steady State

▶ Tinkering: using the Seven S Framework and the TPF Perspective

▶ Tinkering: towards competitive advantage

F. Conclusion

ECM Unit Four

> ❝ Plus ça change, plus c'est la même chose [the more it changes the more it is the same thing].❞
>
> *J.B.A. Karr*[1]

A. Overview

First of all this unit considers the broad strategies behind the development of a business. We focus on a 'steady state' situation, growth and decline or recovery. We put to one side any 'combination' strategies, as most policies will fall in the main into our threefold classification.

Given our themes of enterprise and change, we focus on developing enterprise within these changing environments.

This unit then turns to the steady state scenario. This situation is described and then analysed by use of the Seven S framework, which bridges both external strategy and internal organizational realities.

Once we have a snapshot of this steady state, we begin to tinker with pressures towards change and enterprise. (Non-tinkering changes are covered in Units Five and Six.) Limited enterprise and limited change are used in this unit.

Before we move away from the steady state, vision and performance indicators, or benchmarks, of how to measure the vision are demonstrated.

We use the Seven S and TPF techniques to develop away from the steady state. Finally, the competitive position provides a key backcloth to any development from our three core positions of steady state, growth and decline or recovery, so it is fitting that we conclude the unit with this concept.

B. Generic Strategies

The basic questions managers have to answer in any business are:

- What business are we in?
- Why are we in business?

The first question provides the mission statement and the second question involves setting the objectives.

This approach is developed by Jauch and Glueck,[2] who believe that the first question to be asked needs to clarify the products or services provided, the markets served, and the functions performed. Then, managers should decide how they can develop the business. These authors identify four generic methods for developing a business: **stability** (here called steady state), **expansion** (here called growth), **retrenchment** (here called recovery) and **combination**. The generic methods are based on answers to the following questions:

1 What is our business? What should it be? What business should we be in five years from now? And ten years?

2 Should we stay in the same business(es) with a similar level of effort? (Steady state)

3 Should we turn the enterprise round or get out of the business entirely or some parts of it? (Recovery)

4 Should we expand into new business areas by adding new functions, products and/or markets? (Expansion)

5 Should we carry out alternatives (3) and (4), (2) and (4), or (2) and (3)?

The business may decide to change its functions, markets or products under its current generic strategy, or it may decide to change the effort it is putting into its generic strategy (see figure ECM4.1).

A **steady state** is not a 'do-nothing' approach, and goals such as profits or cash flow are not abandoned. The mission may be stable but the effort involved can be changed to maintain or increase profits and efficiency and

	Growth	**Recovery**	**Steady state**
Products	Add new products or develop new ones	Drop old products or reduce product development	No change except for packaging or quality improvements
Markets	Find new territories or penetrate markets	Drop distribution channels and reduce market share	No change but protect market share and focus on market niches
Functions	Develop vertical integration and/or increase capacity	Sell to one customer and/ or decrease R & D, marketing etc. or lay off employees	No change but improve production efficiency

Figure ECM4.1 Ways in which a firm may change its products, markets or functions according to whether management decides to grow, recover or remain in a steady state.

Source: Adapted from Jauch, L.R., and Glueck, W.F., *Business Policy and Strategic Management* (McGraw-Hill, New York, 1988).

reduce costs. On the other hand, the effort may be maintained but competitive effort is increased in terms of pricing, packaging, segmenting markets, differentiating products, etc.

Businesses in a mature industry or with mature products or services often pursue a policy of stability. Small businesses also frequently adopt this position, and sometimes businesses which are performing erratically decide to follow the steady state approach for a while.

Growth occurs when a business decides to add new products or markets or perhaps integrate backwards and make its own products. Also, the business may increase its efforts to gain market share and expand facilities. High investment and risk taking are implied.

However, although increased assets or size may lead to increased return on investment (ROI), inefficiencies may result. In fact, expansion can be desirable or undesirable, since an expanding business can be inefficient, because the attention of managers is diverted from running the business. There is a general belief that rapid change in the environment demands expansion, which in turn leads to improved performance. This is not always the case.

Recovery occurs when a business has to reduce its products, services, markets or functions and so reduce any negative cash flow. The business often divests itself of products, services, businesses and markets, reduces functions or focuses on fewer customers by withdrawing from distribution. In extreme cases it may be necessary to write off, go bankrupt or realize assets.

Recovery is often reserved for dealing with a crisis and involves abandoning markets, reducing costs and assets, cutting products and increasing cash flow. Such approaches are often useful during the decline stage of a business or industry.

Although perhaps looked on as an admission of failure, a recovery approach can be used to reverse negative trends and set the stage for further development of the business. Therefore, it can be part of a periodic reassessment of the business.

Combination occurs when a business uses the previous methods – steady state, growth and recovery – at the same time or sequentially. Jauch and Glueck believe this approach is not easy to operate and is more common in large, multibusiness organizations during periods of change. So, with our orientation on medium-sized firms, we will focus on the other three generic strategies.

Products/services, markets and functions[3]

Before continuing, you need to be clear about how you define your business in order to decide the way forward. To do this you must clarify the products and/or services provided, the markets served and functions performed. Please tackle Activity ECM4.1.

ACTIVITY ECM4.1

WHERE ARE WE?

Activity code
- ☑ Self-development
- ☑ Teamwork
- ☑ Communications
- ☐ Numeracy/IT
- ☑ Decisions

Task

Determine where 'your' work organization or college is currently 'at'. You or your group could consider such issues as:

- the product or service offered;
- the markets being served;
- the role that your organization seeks to perform.

You should first attempt to pose a range of questions on these topics and then attempt to answer them.

The **product/market matrix** (figure ECM4.2) shows the different ways in which an enterprise could develop. It might choose to stay with its present products and markets and so maintain a stable position. On the other hand, it could expand into related or unrelated products; expand its present product line into more markets; or seek new markets for new products. These approaches are shown in the figure.

Research and observation have shown that the further an enterprise moves from its present products/services and markets, the more risky and unprofitable the move can be.

If necessary, you can alter the products/services you provide, the markets you serve or the functions you perform. You can also increase the level of effort put into these areas and so improve the efficiency and effectiveness of your organization.

Once you have defined your business and you know how it is performing, you have to decide whether to grow, recover, remain in a steady state, or some combination of these. Again, for simplicity we do not tackle the combined strategies.

Now complete Activity ECM4.2.

	Existing products	Related products	New products	
Existing markets	**Low risk** Market penetration	Produce variants or imitations	**High Risk** Extend product line	**Customers** **Forward integration** Transport, distribution channels, customer service
Related markets	Promote aggressively	Segment market Differentiate products	Diversify vertically	
New markets	**High risk** Develop new markets	Expand markets	**Very high risk** Diversify (conglomerate)	

Suppliers
Backward integration
Raw materials, components, plant, equipment

Figure ECM4.2 The product/market matrix and possible approaches to the development of an enterprise.

ACTIVITY ECM4.2

A DEVELOPING MATRIX

Activity code
- ✓ Self-development
- ✓ Teamwork
- ✓ Communications
- ☐ Numeracy/IT
- ✓ Decisions

Task

Using the organization that you identified in Unit One through research, or 'your' work organization or college, tackle the following:

1 Describe 'your' business under the following headings:
  - Products/services
  - Markets
  - Functions
  See Activity ECM4.1

2 Construct a matrix based on figure ECM4.2 and write your present products/services in the box.

3 Identify any related products or markets your enterprise could develop, and insert them into the matrix.
4 In what ways could these be developed?
5 Identify any new products/services or markets your enterprise could develop.
6 In what ways could these be developed?

Variations of the generic strategies

Methods	Growth	Recovery	Steady state
Internal	Penetrate existing markets. Add new products. Add new markets.	Reduce costs and assets. Drop products, markets and functions.	Seek production and marketing efficiency. Reorganize
External	Acquisitions. Mergers.	Divest SBUs. Liquidate. Declare bankrupt.	Maintain market share.
Related	Seek synergy from new products, markets, functions.	Eliminate related products, markets or functions.	Improve products.
Unrelated	Conglomerate diversification in products, markets, functions.	Eliminate unrelated products, markets or functions.	
Vertical	Add new functions.	Reduce functions.	
Offensive	Innovative, entrepreneurial moves.		
Defensive	Imitate in R & D and new products.	Reactive defence of position.	

Figure ECM4.3 Various options available for carrying out the generic strategies.

Source: Adapted from Jauch, L.R. and Glueck, W.F., *Business Policy and Strategic Management* (McGraw-Hill, New York, 1988).

There are several ways in which the generic strategies can be carried out: internally or externally, by related or unrelated development, by horizontal or vertical integration, offensively or defensively. The last two variations will be explained below, but the rest will be explained in Unit Six, since they are more useful for the process of expanding an enterprise. The variation chosen will depend on the internal strengths and weaknesses of the business, the opportunities and threats offered by the environment and the preferences of the management. These methods are summarized in figure ECM4.3.

Offensive and defensive variations
Some approaches to attack and to defence can be seen in Box ECM4.1 and Box ECM4.2.

BOX ECM4.1

Offensive variations

According to Thompson and Strickland, there are six ways to mount offensives:[1]

1 Attack competitors' strengths.
2 Attack competitors' weaknesses.
3 Attack on many fronts simultaneously.
4 First-mover offensives.
5 Guerrilla attacks.
6 Pre-emptive strikes.

Whom should you attack?

- market leaders
- runner-up firms
- struggling firms
- small local and regional firms.

Offensives depend on competitive advantages such as:

- lower-cost products;
- changes in production that lower costs or enhance differentiation;
- superior performance or lower user costs;
- more responsive after-sales support;
- a new distribution channel;
- selling direct to users.

Offensives are dependent on what the organization does best:

- its competitive strengths or capabilities;
- key skills or strong functional competencies (the value chain is important here too).

The timing of offensives is just as important to success as the move itself. Making the first move is best when:

- it builds image and reputation;

- there are early commitments to raw materials, new technology, distribution channels, etc., which can provide a cost advantage;
- first-time customers can remain loyal to pioneering firms when making repeat purchases;
- it is a pre-emptive strike which makes imitation hard or unlikely.

The disadvantages for the first mover are:

- pioneering leadership can be costly and the experience curve effects negligible;
- technological change is so rapid that early investments are soon obsolete;
- customer loyalty to pioneering firms can be weak;
- skills and knowhow developed by pioneers can be copied easily by late movers.

Source:

1 Thompson, A.A. and Strickland, A.J. *Strategic Management: concepts and cases* (Irwin, Holmewood, IL, 1992).

BOX ECM4.2

Defensive variations

Thompson and Strickland believe defensive moves lower the risk of being attacked, weaken the impact of an attack when it occurs, and cause potential attackers to choose someone else.[1] Such variations may not increase a firm's competitive advantage but they do help to sustain and strengthen those it has.

An organization can protect its competitive position as follows:

- Block any possibilities for being attacked by presenting a moving target rather than protecting the status quo. A good defence involves adjusting quickly to changing industry conditions and being the first mover in any situation.
- Signal that you will retaliate strongly if attacked. This dissuades attackers from attacking or diverts them to attack other competitors.
- Reduce your margins or use accounting methods that do not expose your profitability.

Source:

1 Thompson, A.A. and Strickland, A.J., *Strategic Management: concepts and cases* (Irwin, Holmewood, IL, 1992).

Choosing your generic strategy

Assuming some free choice (which may be a big assumption), to help you to decide the generic strategy to use, whether growth, steady state or recovery, it may be useful to analyse your enterprise using Lewin's force field approach. As we have noted in Unit One, Lewin[4] developed a way of looking at change called 'force field analysis', which envisages change as a dynamic balance of forces working in opposite directions at any particular point in time. This means that any situation is in a state of equilibrium as a result of forces pushing against one another. The forces pushing for change are balanced by those resisting change.

Whether or not we have such a free choice, the situation that we find ourselves in can still be analysed using this methodology (see figure ECM4.4).

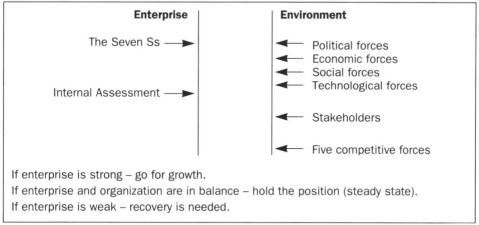

Figure ECM4.4 Forces between an enterprise and its environment in a force field diagram.

Thus, in order to make a change a manager has to modify the current balance of forces by:

■ increasing the strength of enterprise;

■ reducing or removing the environmental forces;

■ moving the direction of a force.

Please tackle Activity ECM4.3.

ACTIVITY ECM4.3

GENERIC METHODS

Activity code
- ✓ Self-development
- ✓ Teamwork
- ✓ Communications
- ✓ Numeracy/IT
- ✓ Decisions

Tasks

Using 'your' organization (see Activity ECM4.2), you should now be able to answer the following questions based on the work you have done to date:

1 What is your business?
   What should it be?
   What business should you be in five years from now? And ten years?
2 Should you stay in the same business with the same level of effort? (Steady state)
3 Should you turnaround or get out of the business or parts of it? (Recovery)
4 Should you expand by adding new products/ services, markets or functions? (Growth)

A report is required (1,000 words maximum).

For the rest of the book we shall adopt a model for an ideal situation: steady state, recovery or growth. An organization may find itself in one of these situations either by choice or by accident. We should now be able to determine which situation the organization is in at the present time, based on the work we have done so far in this unit and in Units Two and Three. Once we understand the model, we should be able to understand the effect of change on the model and ways of changing one scenario into another through enterprise.

C. Steady State

Introduction

All organizations change in the long term, but in the short term there may be no good reason for changing the role an organization performs or altering its products/services or markets. The objective is to make profits from doing things better rather than investing heavily in growth. Disadvantages could be the possibility of being overtaken by new developments and a lack of development opportunities for managers. Now please read some reasons for maintaining a steady state (Box ECM4.3) and tackle Activity ECM4.4.

BOX ECM4.3

Maintaining a steady state

Luffman et al. give the following reasons for maintaining a steady state:[1]

- to maintain market share in the early stages of a product life cycle may be the best way of using resources.
- The risks associated with expansion may be greater than the expected returns.
- The cash resources may not be available.

Source:
1 Adapted from Luffman, G., Sanderson, S., Lea, E. and Kenny, B., Business Policy: an analytical introduction (Blackwell Publishers, Oxford, 1987).

ACTIVITY ECM4.4

A STEADY STATE

Activity code
✓ Self-development
☐ Teamwork
☐ Communications
☐ Numeracy/IT
✓ Decisions

Task

While noting the work of Luffman et al. (see Box ECM4.3), indicate other reasons why organizations may wish to pursue a 'steady state' policy.

In general, a steady state is most successful in a mature industry and in a slowly changing environment. When the major competitors are satisfied with modest returns, rivalry and threats from substitutes are low and the power of buyers and suppliers is acceptable.

Many managers ask why, if an enterprise is successful, they should risk failure by making changes. By waiting, the enterprise can learn from the mistakes of others before making any necessary change. On the other hand, the enterprise may need a period of stability following one of major change in order to regain some control.

By following a policy of stability, managers may become too complacent and the external environment may change without stimulating the necessary response of enterprise. It may be too late for enterprise to capitalize on new opportunities, or the threats may have become real before enterprise can react. Therefore, a steady state approach must involve an effective system for monitoring change in the environment, and it necessitates managers who are able to determine the right time to respond to the environment.

Essentially a steady state implies few major changes to the organization's role, products/services or markets. The organization concentrates its resources where it can sustain the best competitive advantage. This is not a 'do-nothing' approach, since continuous improvement in performance should be a major objective for any manager. This can be achieved by greater efficiency; reduced costs; improved quality; increased prices; improved human relations; rationalized production, products and markets; improved organizational structure; and deeper penetration of the same markets with the same products, etc.

The steady state scenario

The suggested scenario may be something like the following outline.

A relative calm prevails. Politically, a stable democracy exists, and on the economic front demand is steady. The organization is ahead of its rivals and there are no entrants of significance. Even if there are new entrants, they would take time to catch up. Social changes are of course occurring, but they do not have a great impact on the labour force, suppliers or customers. Technically, innovations are ticking over in the sector. The external environment is therefore stable and the organization is in a 'steady state' rather than in a mode of expansion or contraction.

Complete Activity ECM4.5 before you go any further, then write the report for Activity ECM4.6.

ACTIVITY ECM4.5

MASS TRANSIT SYSTEM LIMITED (MTSL)

Activity code

☑ Self-development
☑ Teamwork
☑ Communications
☐ Numeracy/IT
☑ Decisions

MTSL has to provide a safe, economic and efficient transport system for a city and can be considered to be operating in a steady state. There are probably six key stakeholders for MTSL:

1 **Government**   This funds one-third of the expenditure on core activities as well as work on new lines and extensions. The government also influences MTSL through regulations, taxation and economic policies.

2 **Customers**   Without customers MTSL cannot exist as a business, as two-thirds of its income is derived from customers using the system. Customers are able to exert pressure through the MTSL Passengers' Committee.

3 **Employees**   MTSL is only able to achieve its objectives through the actions of its employees. Employees work to satisfy their own personal, social and economic needs. Therefore the challenge for employer–employee relations is to create a situation in which both parties achieve their goals together. Employees are able to exert influence by taking part in employee satisfaction surveys and by being members of trade unions.

4 **Competition**   MTSL holds a monopoly since no other organization operates an underground system. Nevertheless, it still has to compete with other public transport providers such as buses, the railway, taxis and the private car. There is a special relationship with the railway and bus networks.

5 **Suppliers**   It is in the interest of MTSL to maintain good relationships with its suppliers.

6 **Local communities**   The local community is the source for labour, customers and capital. It influences MTSL through the Customer Charter and regular borough liaison meetings.

MTSL can exert influence on these stakeholders by lobbying; holding frequent meetings with interested parties; coalitions with other groups, such as the International Union of Public Transport or the Community of European Railways; or deliberately leaking information to the media to gain support.

MTSL has separate directorates responsible for specific areas of business and for monitoring parts of the environment:

- The Communications Directorate monitors the local community and government.
- The Development Directorate monitors the technological and economic environments.
- The Passenger Services Directorate monitors the customer and government environments.
- The Engineering Directorate monitors the technological and supplier environments.
- The Railway Extensions Directorate monitors government, technological and ecological environments.
- The Safety and Quality Directorate monitors government, ecological and technological environments.
- The Finance and Business Planning Directorate monitors customer, competition and economic environments.
- The Human Resources Directorate monitors the labour market and government environments.

The Finance and Business Planning Directorate has the responsibility for monitoring and analysing the customer and competitor environments for the other directorates.

The research and other information gathered by these directorates is then developed to provide a number of products for use by MTSL managers for service and investment planning. The information is communicated in several ways:

- *Customer News* is produced four times per year and sent to all employees in order to focus efforts on providing customer benefits.
- Quarterly or six-monthly presentations are made to the various management groups in order to ensure that research is regularly discussed throughout the business.
- Research reports are produced to bring together research in key areas.
- Business case manuals are produced for the professional planners.
- Key performance indicators (KPIs) information packs are produced for the Passenger Services Directorate to help them plan operating activities and the achievement of KPIs.

There is obviously plenty of information to enable MTSL to respond to its environment and develop long-term strategies. The fact that it is available, however, does not guarantee that it is used effectively.

Task

Discuss the various ways of ensuring that the information collected about the environment is used effectively.

ACTIVITY ECM4.6

YOUR CURRENT POSITION

Activity code

☑ Self-development
☑ Teamwork
☑ Communications
☑ Numeracy/IT
☑ Decisions

Tasks

Your managing director has asked you to determine whether 'your' organization is in a steady state, recovery or growth situation. Write a 500-word report setting out the position based on your analysis of the situation.

You could examine:

■ the **external environment**, using a PEST analysis, the five competitive forces, an industry analysis and a stakeholder analysis;

■ the **internal environment**, using a financial analysis, the Seven S Framework and the value chain.

The PEST analysis

This will enable you to determine the opportunities and threats facing your organization.

■ Is it possible to change some of the threats into opportunities?

■ Can you prioritize the opportunities and threats or decide whether they are short-term or long-term?

The five competitive forces

This analysis will enable you to decide your strengths and weaknesses in the marketplace. What needs to be done to improve your position?

The industry analysis

This will enable you to determine your position in the industry. What needs to be done to improve your position?

The stakeholder analysis

This will enable you to determine the stakeholders that are the key to the success of your organization.

The financial analysis

This will focus your attention on the financial strengths and weaknesses of your organization.

The Seven S Framework
This will help you to determine whether there is synergy between the Seven Ss. Do they complement one another or are one or two out of balance?

The value chain
This will focus your attention on the areas of the business in which you can gain competitive advantage.

If you conclude that 'your' organization is in a steady state, you should stay with this unit, whereas if 'your' organization is in a recovery situation you may wish to go to Unit Five; and if 'your' organization is growing fast, you may wish to turn to Unit Six.

Knowledge and awareness of all three states are still useful in understanding 'your' current position.

An analysis of the steady state: the Seven S Framework

Strategy

Several words such as 'consolidation', 'neutral', 'defensive' and 'stability' have been used in the literature to describe the steady state approach to managing a business. A steady state occurs when there is no significant deviation from previous business policies. The organization continues with the same products/services, markets and functions as in its business definition. It tends to focus on an incremental improvement in functional performance. In those cases where an organization has found a formula for success, changing that formula without good reason may be a mistake. On the other hand, continuing with the formula that brought success in the past has dangers, particularly where the environment may be changing radically.

Nevertheless, as we have noted, a steady state is not a 'do-nothing' approach, since it can be designed to increase profits through increasing the efficiency in current operations. There may be no change in the products/services, markets or functions but the effort put into them may be increased. There may also be pricing or packaging changes to protect market share. You can grow with the market, place more emphasis on quality of product or service, increase marketing activity, improve cost structure through productivity gains and/or higher capital intensity, etc.

If a business wishes to continue with its current products and markets, the position in the life cycle of the product or market must be examined. There is, however, the problem of measuring the growth rates for determining this position. If you take revenue you have the problem of inflation, so units sold may be a better indicator.

When a market is growing the choice of the steady state option implies that the business must grow at the same rate to retain its market share. If the market share drops then the cost structure could be higher than competitors'. This means that investment in equipment, marketing, people, etc., must keep pace with the growth.

When a market is mature the reduced rate of growth requires less investment and competition stabilizes. This situation necessitates segmenting the market and utilizing assets efficiently in order to maximize ROI.

Organizations in the mature state of development or in a mature market may be expected to operate in this way and so maintain a comfortable market or profit position. Sometimes this approach can be used to bring a business with widely fluctuating results under control.

To recap on the strategic format, there are several reasons for operating a steady state approach:

- The organization perceives it is successful.
- It is easier, more comfortable and less risky.
- The management is action-oriented.
- The environment is perceived to be stable.
- Expansion can lead to inefficiencies.
- Expansion cannot continue indefinitely.
- The organization only has the resources to continue with the current approach.
- The organization's goals are satisfied by the current approach.
- The culture of the organization is set in its ways.

Structure

In this situation there may be a functional structure which is centralized. The structure is supportive of the calm organization but can be rather bureaucratic, with perhaps too much slack. There is normally no change needed in the reporting structure and the way tasks are divided up and integrated. The problem is how to make the structure work efficiently and effectively.

As we have noted, Burns and Stalker[5] found that a mechanistic structure was more suited to a stable environment whereas an organic structure was more suited to a turbulent one. Lawrence and Lorsch[6] found that those firms operating in an unstable environment were the most highly differentiated and those operating in a stable environment were least differentiated. In both types of environment, high-performing organizations had a higher degree of integration than the low performers. Morse and Lorsch[7] found that the structures of the most effective departments in an organization fitted their environment, while the structures of the least effective did not.

Systems

These can become a fetish, since systems for control, information and intelligence seem to have lives of their own. There is often considerable investment and reinvestment in information technology. Do the systems support the structure? Look for increased efficiency and effectiveness. Information, capital budgeting, manufacturing, quality and performance measurement systems, etc., need to be examined

Please read Box ECM4.4.

BOX ECM4.4

Monitoring systems in government

The Department of National Heritage (DNH) is a small, policy-oriented government department with responsibility for the built heritage, museums and galleries, the Sports Council, libraries, the living arts, broadcasting and the press, sport, tourism and the National Lottery. It has two executive agencies, the Historical Royal Palaces Agency and the Royal Parks Agency. Thus, the DNH works with or through organizations, including forty-three non-departmental public bodies (NDPBs), which operate at arm's length from government. Each of these organizations is unique and makes an important contribution to the quality of life of the nation. The DNH was set up to provide leadership and guidance on the government's objectives and priorities, and to assist with providing funds and support for these sectors.

There are three monitoring systems in operation:

1 The Press Office operates both proactively and reactively. Proactively, the DNH provides news releases which are sent to news editors as a result of a ministerial statement or keynote address. Reactively, the DNH monitors the national press and sends information to the minister's office and the various divisions.

2 The Implementation and Review Team monitors and reports on DNH progress in securing better value for money and better public services by expanding competition. The Review Team constantly monitors the effects of market testing. The NDPBs have their own monitoring systems in place and are required to provide returns to DNH to show how they are meeting the requirements of the Citizen's Charter.

   The team also monitors the internal 'Green Housekeeping Strategy', and external monitoring of green issues occurs within divisions, such as those for tourism and sports.

3 The Personnel Division monitors public-sector pay and the response of the NDH to the Investors in People Initiative, which is the new national standard to help British business get the most out of its people.

Style

The predominant approach is reasonably relaxed, being neither hard nor soft. The management style fits with a stable approach. Leadership and management behaviour match the steady state.

Staff
The employees of the enterprise from top management downwards provide a pool of resources to be nurtured, developed, guarded and allocated. There is a continuous need to strengthen training and development for everyone. Demographic impact on skills and appraisal, rewards, motivation, morale, attitudes and behaviour may need maintenance. There is a solid employer image, rather ceremonial and a little too 'fat', perhaps. Overall, it looks to be quite comfortable.

Skills
Human resources management is often strong. There is a lot of training and development going on, although not necessarily related to business needs. There is a need to weed out old skills and supporting structures and systems to ensure new skills can take root and grow.

Shared values
There is room for a more pluralistic viewpoint rather than a 'pure' managerial perspective. The culture of the organization fits with a stable approach.

D. Change and Enterprise

If events move quickly, the steady state may become increasingly redundant – if it is not overturned by external and internal changes. Consequently, enterprise and change management may become very significant. If things become worse, the discussion in Unit Five may have relevance. If things become far better, Unit Six may be relevant. Let us be neither pessimistic nor optimistic and assume some limited growth or development.

Before considering this development away from the steady state, some common denominators of movement away from any of the three states may be worthwhile examining. We will consider the vision, performance objectives and competitive advantage.

The vision

We are not in charge of our own destiny, but we can have a vision, a view of where we would like to be, a creative feel of where the organization should be heading over the next five or ten years.

Developing a vision is a creative act which can be based on some of the analysis to date. Essentially, managers should try to identify a new future that can be communicated both inside and outside the organization. The organization responds by developing its resources to achieve that vision. Please read Box ECM4.5 for a definition of a vision statement. Then tackle Activity ECM4.7.

BOX ECM4.5

The vision or mission statement

According to Rowe et al., a vision statement needs to be:[1]

- simple, clear and easily understood;
- possessed of an envisaged future that looks far enough ahead to allow for dramatic changes but close enough to attract commitment from employees;
- able to focus the organization on the right things at the right time;
- frequently articulated, to gain a consensus that the vision is desirable and attainable.

The following definitions may be useful:

- **Vision** is a statement of where the organization is heading over the next five or ten years.
- **Mission** is the purpose of the organization – why it is in business, what it does and whom it serves. Good mission statements enable employees to develop loyalty and direction from a common purpose.
- **Values** are the broad beliefs about what is or what is not done in or by the organization. The corporate culture is the value system for the organization as a whole.

Useful topics for consideration are:

- commitment to quality;
- commitment to innovation;
- duty to and respect for employees;
- duty to shareholders;
- duty to suppliers;
- importance of ethical standards;
- importance of honesty and integrity;
- importance of protecting the environment;
- importance of corporate citizenship and social responsibility.

Source:

1 Rowe, A.J., Mason, R.O., Dickel, K.E. and Snyder, N.H., *Strategic Management: a methodological approach* (Addison-Wesley, Reading, MA, 1990).

ACTIVITY ECM4.7

I HAD A DREAM

Activity code
☑ Self-development
☐ Teamwork
☑ Communications
☐ Numeracy/IT
☑ Decisions

Task

Write a 250-word report to your board setting out your proposal for the vision of 'your' organization. This can be on the organization you have researched or your own workplace or college.

Performance objectives and milestones

Once the vision has been decided, the methods of achieving it have to be worked out. This means defining objectives. The vision statement must be converted into specific performance objectives that enable managers to evaluate performance. Objectives define what managers are committed to produce in a particular time period and so direct attention to what needs to be done.

Objectives are required for two major types of key result areas, financial and strategic:

1 **Financial objectives** tend to be short-term and include revenue and earnings growth, dividend rates, profit margins, returns on investment, credit ratings, cash flow, share price, etc.

2 **Strategic objectives** tend to be long-term and include market share, industry ranking, product/service quality, low relative costs, product line breadth and attractiveness, leadership in technology and innovation, ability to compete regionally, nationally, globally, etc.

Which of these two groups of objectives take priority? Perhaps the Japanese point the way when they gain market share at the expense of short-term profits, whereas many western firms have mainly pursued short-term profits and neglected their long-term future. On the other hand, letting your competitors know your objectives enables them to develop their objectives, which may defeat you.

The strategic objectives set out the organization's business position or strategic intent.[8] Most organizations which become successful set themselves strategic intentions that are out of all proportion to their current capability or market position. They pursue their long-term objectives relentlessly over perhaps ten or twenty years. Komatsu set out to beat Caterpillar, Cannon to beat Xerox, Walmart to beat Sears, and so on. Such long-term battle-cries can focus the efforts of the organization far better than the detailed strategic plans coming out of ivory towers.

The objectives often result from the expectations and power of individuals, coalitions and stakeholders. Organizations require several objectives to satisfy their vision statement and these are often separated into **short-** and **long-term objectives**. Managers are often pressured into short-term objectives, but these can have a severe impact on the long-term success or even survival of the organization.

The long-term objectives focus attention on what is required to be done now in order to achieve the long-term objective. At the same time, managers are forced to examine their short-term objectives in order to determine what effect they will have on long-term performance. To summarize the point: short-term objectives should be stepping stones to long-term objectives.

These objectives also have to be prioritized and measured in terms of efficiency or effectiveness. (To remind you: efficiency is the ratio of inputs to outputs, whereas effectiveness is the degree of achievement of the objective relative to some standard.) Sometimes there must be a trade-off between efficiency and effectiveness.

The objectives should be challenging but attainable and should cascade down through the organization in a way that ensures goal congruence between its various parts. Box ECM4.6 gives a 'feel' for the objectives of a typical engineering company.

BOX ECM4.6

Typical performance objectives

Financial objectives

- Achieve a minimum after-tax return on capital employed of 14 per cent.
- Achieve a return on shareholders' equity through a capital structure including 25–35 per cent debt.
- Achieve a minimum return on equity of 18 per cent.
- Pay dividends equal to approximately 40 per cent of earnings.
- Achieve average annual growth in earnings of at least 10 per cent.

Operating objectives

- Have a leading market share position in our major markets.
- Be recognized as a leader in the application of technology to meet customer requirements.
- Be a 'best-value' supplier throughout the world.
- Expand our international business to a level equalling 20–25 per cent of company sales.
- Invest in research and development at a rate of 4 per cent of sales as a means of achieving our market leadership objectives.

Human resource objectives

- Encourage initiative, innovation and productivity by appropriately recognizing and rewarding employee performance.
- Invest in employee training and development at a rate of 2 per cent of payroll.
- Honestly and accurately appraise and evaluate the performance of each employee on at least an annual basis.
- Provide for orderly succession in management.
- Maintain a positive action programme and provide employees with the opportunity for advancement commensurate with their abilities.

Social/community responsibility

- Maintain a safe, clean and healthy environment for our employees and the communities in which we operate.
- Invest 1.5 per cent of net income in social, cultural, educational and charitable activities.
- Encourage appropriate employee involvement in community activities.

Quite often there is a difference between official objectives and actual objectives. Official objectives are those which the organization says it seeks whereas actual objectives are those which it puts money and time into. Managers should be aware of this dichotomy and the effect it may have on stakeholders.

Management by objectives (MbO) can be used to develop an organization's philosophy to encourage managers to define their objectives in formal, specific, time-based, prioritized, measurable terms which are challenging but attainable.

Some managers tend to resist being specific about objectives, since they claim that this reduces flexibility and prevents them from exploring new ideas. However, without finite objectives it may be difficult to improve each of our three scenarios.

Furthermore, the notion of competitive advantage is critical in explaining possible degrees of development in each of our three scenarios. A more limited use of such advantage may prevail under the steady state scenario and alongside possible marginal moves away from the relative equilibrium of the steady state position.

Competitive advantage: seeking and maintaining

Porter believes organizations can sustain their competitive advantage, lower the risk of being attacked, weaken any attack and deflect any attacks on to competitors by:[9]

- broadening the firm's product line to close off vacant niches and gaps to would-be challenges;
- introducing models or brands that match the characteristics competitors' models have or might have;
- keeping prices low on models that closely resemble those of competitors;
- signing exclusive agreements with dealers and distributors to keep competitors from using the same ones;
- granting dealers and distributors large discounts to discourage them from experimenting with other suppliers;
- offering free or low-cost training to buyer's personnel;
- making it harder for competitors to get buyers to try their brands by:
  - giving discounts to buyers who are considering rival brands;
  - resorting to high levels of coupon offers and free samples;
  - making early announcements about new products or price changes so that buyers think twice about switching;
- raising the amount of financing offered to dealers and/or buyers;
- reducing delivery times for spare parts;
- increasing warranty values;
- patenting alternative technologies;
- protecting knowhow in products, production and other parts of the activity-cost chain;
- signing exclusive contracts with the best suppliers;
- purchasing natural resource reserves ahead of current needs;
- avoiding suppliers that also serve competitors;
- challenging competitors' products or practices in the courts;
- publicly announcing management commitment to maintaining the present market share;
- publicly announcing plans to construct adequate production capacity to meet forecast demand or building ahead of demand;
- providing advance information about new products, technology, brands or models;
- publicly committing the firm to a policy of matching the prices or terms offered by competitors;
- maintaining a reserve of cash and marketable securities;
- making an occasional strong response to the moves of weak competitors in order to discourage them.

Please read Box ECM4.7 and Box ECM4.8.

BOX ECM4.7

Engineering an exit: an example

When General Electric sold its computing business to Honeywell in 1970 it also sold a 66 per cent interest in Compagnie des Machines Bull. This gave Honeywell access to both USA and continental markets and produced Honeywell Information Systems (HIS) Inc. During the 1970s, Honeywell attempted to strengthen its position in the computer industry through a series of acquisitions, mergers and collaborative agreements.

By 1980, it became obvious to Honeywell's management that although they were still making profits they were not going to be able to maintain the market share of 6 per cent which they had had in the 1970s. Honeywell were beginning to look for a way out of the computer industry. The new computer family of 1982 targeted market niches rather than competing head on with IBM across the whole range of computers.

The year 1984 saw Honeywell Information Systems make a ten-year agreement with NEC of Japan for the manufacture and distribution rights of the NEC mainframe. However, by 1986 Honeywell had decided that the best way to protect their current customers while avoiding selling their assets would be a strategic alliance with Bull and NEC. This created the first computer company jointly owned by European, Japanese and USA companies. The three partners had an interest in the computer industry but little else in common in terms of national culture, economic and political objectives, and company structures.

Key issues included choosing a name for the new company which reflected the needs of each member of the alliance, and so Honeywell Bull was born. The parts of the business which belonged to Honeywell Information Systems (HIS) and Honeywell itself had to be sorted out. In general the employees of HIS became employees of Honeywell Bull, but a new management team was installed and the headquarters located at Minneapolis. New employee benefits and incentives had to be negotiated, since these varied from one subsidiary to another.

The management team that took over on 27 March 1987 had to turn around an established, bureaucratic organization, plus R & D, purchasing, production, sales and service organizations across the globe. The board of French, Japanese and Americans had to learn to work together within a framework of blocking rights. There were obvious opportunities for synergy in production, technology and R & D. However, Honeywell Bull began with the excess capacity and marketing, sales and services which were not able to take up the slack. Facing them they had the might of IBM, DEC and Unisys.

Source:

Adapted from J. Roos, *Co-operative Strategies* (Prentice Hall, Hemel Hempstead, 1994).

BOX ECM4.8

Shipbuilding torpedoed despite the Cold War ending

The tragedy that has befallen Swan Hunter has demonstrated the consequences of ministers having no strategy to manage change.[1]

The 'Great' in 'Great Britain' was based partly on its economic strength, derived from its industrial base, its commercial acumen, its military power and its naval and seafaring domination of the waters of the world. This maritime expertise was related to its shipbuilding capacity.

During the last twenty or so years, there has been considerable fallout in UK shipbuilding, with leaner and hungrier companies left in the market. Japan has some 33 per cent of the industry, Korea has 20 per cent and Britain has fallen to thirteenth in the world supply league.

Not only that, but the industry has been geared to production of warships in the context of the Cold War. With the demise of the Cold War (certainly in the early 1990s, although Russian imperialism may resurface), the industry needs to change direction to non-naval status. However, governmental blocs at national and European level seem to be unable to see this writing on the wall.

The speed of the collapse of the Eastern bloc may have shocked most of us, but policies built on the status quo with no in-built mechanisms for change can only mean decline – if not despair. Government, particularly in this case, has a key role to play.

Source:

1 Adapted from Dromey, J. 'An industry vanishes down the slipway', *Guardian*, 24 June (1993).

E. Developing the Steady State

Tinkering: using the Seven S Framework and the TPF Perspective

Let us assume that we want to tinker with the steady state. The external environment may be altering slightly or a more enterprising management may be seeking greater opportunities – although this is not a drive for rapid growth.

Please refer to Activity ECM4.8. Once it is completed, read Box ECM4.9.

ACTIVITY ECM4.8

TINKERING

Activity code
☑ Self-development
☑ Teamwork
☑ Communications
☐ Numeracy/IT
☑ Decisions

Task

Using the Seven S approach outlined in this section, how would you or your group fine-tune the steady state?

Once you (or your group) have completed this activity, refer to Box ECM4.9 for an indicative response.

BOX ECM4.9

Tinkering with the Seven Ss in the steady state

Strategy
It is ticking over and the overall policy is 'more of the same'. Perhaps heavier marketing promotion would maintain and further the organization's presence.

Structure
A tightening up of the job responsibilities and of the reporting relationships may give greater efficiency with less duplication of effort and more individual and functional focus.

Systems
The end-use value of the internal and external management information systems may need to be examined so that the means (technology, systems) does not dictate the ends (business intelligence, results).

Style
The style is seen to be working, so no fundamental change is required. Indeed, the style is seen as a positive plus at the moment.

Staff

Overstaffing and job duplication may be a problem here. While not turning the world upside down, tighter recruitment and selection, derived from an ongoing staffing plan, may be the order of the day. Greater emphasis on productivity with cost-cutting schemes and incentive bonuses may be used to maintain the steady state.

Skills

The predominant skills are adequate, but training almost for its own sake should not be occurring. A thorough training needs analysis seems to be on the cards.

Shared values

The pluralistic vision is more than working and the managerial tolerance of different philosophies – from employees, for example – continues. This tolerance becomes stretched in times of collective labour conflict.

Let us assume now that we want to develop away from the steady state. We do not want to go backwards, so we are assuming some limited growth.

Please refer to Activity ECM4.9. Once it is completed, read Box ECM4.10.

ACTIVITY ECM4.9

GROWTH AND THE TPF TECHNIQUE

Activity code

☑ Self-development
☑ Teamwork
☑ Communications
☐ Numeracy/IT
☑ Decisions

Task

As we have used the Seven S approach earlier, we will switch to the TPF technique here. You may wish to develop the Seven S approach in this context as well.)

Assuming limited growth, using the TPF Perspective, outline the implications of greater change awareness and of a more enterprising organization.

BOX ECM4.10

Developing the steady state: the TPF technique

The current situation needs to be 'moved on' in order to enhance enterprise and the capacity for change.

Element	Current	Proposed
Task		
Planning	The time scales are long – five to ten years; not much scope for more reactive plans.	The planning time span is too long. It needs some built-in flexibility with, say, five-year plans, modified by annual plans.
Goals	These exist but they are not too onerous at departmental or job level.	These goals must be streamlined to give focus to individual departments – if not functions (see later).
Control	Management is in control due to the lack of change.	A 'fat cat' philosophy may prevail here. The variables can change quickly though, so monitoring and intelligence systems are paramount to give early warning. Whether or not the adaptability is here is debatable – even when the information on the environment is received.
Decision-making	This tends to become routine.	There is a case for developing more creative approaches to decision making through training and brainstorming sessions, because non-routine decisions may be required and the 'play-it-safe' approach used to date may not be enough.
Co-ordination	A lot of work goes into making resources for the organization. Duplication of effort exists.	A tightening up of resource allocation and deployment looks long overdue.

Element	Current	Proposed
People		
Motivation	A lot of employee complaints exist but the workforce is loyal and the labour turnover is marginal. The rewards are reasonable and above the going rate.	The employees are grudgingly loyal and the incentive and motivation strategies need to be revamped – for example, job design.
Leadership	This looks to be absent.	Leadership training is required.
Communications	Given the scale of the organization, communications can be difficult. Short cuts develop and the heavy load of information may mean key factors are not given due managerial attention.	At one level this means finer tuning of systems, but at the interpersonal level there is a case for a communications audit.
Functions	These tend to be operations-led; strong on research but light on marketing; conscious of costs, but possibly neglecting finance – for example, in investment appraisal.	Accounting and operations dominate at the expense of marketing, finance (for instance, investment appraisal) and people. The marketing orientation needs to be greater to meet the needs of enterprise.

Tinkering: towards competitive advantage

The mild tinkering approach is epitomized by the Morgan Motor Company Ltd (see Activity ECM4.10). However, most organizations will have to seek greater degrees of competitive advantage to sustain longer term health. Please complete Activity ECM4.11.

ACTIVITY ECM4.10

THE MORGAN MOTOR COMPANY LIMITED

Activity code

☑ Self-development

☐ Teamwork

☐ Communications

☐ Numeracy/IT

☑ Decisions

The Morgan Motor Company is the world's oldest privately owned manufacturer, founded in 1909 by H.F.S. Morgan, who designed the innovative Morgan three-wheeler. Nearly nine decades later, the Morgan Motor Company is still a pioneer and is breaking new boundaries in its own individual way.

Demand for Morgans currently outstrips supply and as a result depreciation is not a word normally used in conjunction with Morgans. Like many handbuilt products, a Morgan is an object of value unaffected by passing fashions.

But traditional craftsmanship does not imply antiquated performance. Morgans provide the sheer thrill of driving a car that is fast and responsive, like a thoroughbred animal. This is what makes a Morgan so special, what creates 'Morgan Magic'.

The development of the Morgan car itself continues all the time. To stay ahead of our competitors in performance and reliability, improvements in design are vital.

The changes that the company makes to the design of the car are the responsibility of people, not committees, and customer feedback is an essential element of future changes in design. The flexibility of our manufacturing process allows us to incorporate many of your requirements in the design and build of your car.

The above extracts from the 1994 Morgan brochure provide a flavour of a small, family-owned motor company. Indeed, they still think of themselves as 'coachbuilders and motor engineers', a description from the early years of this century.

However, a few years ago Harvey-Jones visited Morgan as part of the BBC *Troubleshooter* series. He found a company which was rather antiquated and barely making a profit, but with owners who were happy in what they were doing. Peter Morgan's philosophy was to build a sports car at a price a 'reasonable man' could afford to pay, and he saw himself as in the motor car business rather than in the search for profit. In fact, Morgan shunned growth for growth's sake.

Particular problems highlighted were the low production figures and confused production system; the widespread use of hand tools and antiquated machinery; high stock levels and low profits. Some of these problems seem to be being addressed, since the brochure implies that production processes are being resituated to be at the best points for efficient assembly.

For many years and through several economic depressions they have had an order book of five or more years, and this makes them fairly impregnable. The demand is based on very little advertising and a few distributors both nationally and worldwide. Morgan support circuit racing in both the UK and Germany, and also hill-climb and sprint championships through the British Morgan Sports Car Club, with associated clubs throughout the world. 'The feeling of being part of a large family of Morgan owners is synonymous with owning a Morgan.'

Here we have a company which does not wish to grow or make large profits and yet has the potential to live forever.

Task

Compare and contrast the philosophy expressed by Morgan Cars with that of most managers, who wish to grow and make large profits.

ACTIVITY ECM4.11

COMPETITIVE ADVANTAGE

Activity code
- ☑ Self-development
- ☐ Teamwork
- ☑ Communications
- ☐ Numeracy/IT
- ☑ Decisions

Task

Given your knowledge of the Seven S and TPF techniques in attempting to move the steady state along gently, determine the implications of this movement in Porter's list of typical features of competitive advantage. (Refer back to the section of this unit on 'Competitive advantage: seeking and maintaining' to determine which features are relevant to our current needs.)

F. Conclusion

Any significant external change will have serious ramifications on this sleepy scenario of the steady state. Internally, a lack of enterprise and incapability of change may spell disaster. The internal environment will not be able to cope with change or with real enterprise.

If the internal equilibrium is changed (via the Seven S or TPF techniques), management may have greater vision and linked performance objectives, which may cement themselves to strategic awareness to gain competitive advantage. Even if no radical change from external sources occurs, fine-tuning of the internal organization will be required to allow the steady state scenario to continue. This fine-tuning can be adjusted through the Seven S technique or the TPF approach linked to strategic awareness.

Those managers who can see the possibility of the steady state falling into a decline should look at Unit Five, where the principles of recovery are outlined. If managers can see the possibilities for growth, then Unit Six outlines the principles to follow for growth.

To conclude, the steady state scenario is not one of an organization on its deathbed; it is one of 'ticking over'. Sometimes this can be maintained for some time, but environments are ever changing and every threatening. There may also be a need for greater initiative and enterprise. Either way, to maintain some form of equilibrium, fine-tuning of the Seven S or TPF features alongside overall policy will be required. If the equilibrium alters more radically, even greater strategic awareness and enterprising action will be needed, alongside internal organizational changes. This touches upon vision and objectives.

So the steady state does imply movement: far from this state it is far easier for the organization to go into rapid decline. We turn to this scenario in the next unit.

Notes

1 Karr, J.B.A., *Les Guêpes* (1849).
2 Jauch, L.R. and Glueck, W.F., *Business Policy and Strategic Management* (McGraw-Hill, New York, 1988).
3 This section is based on Porter, M.E., *Competitive Strategy: techniques for analyzing industries and competitors* (Free Press, New York, 1980).
4 Lewin, K., *Field Theory in Social Science* (Harper and Rowe, New York, 1951).
5 Burns, T. and Stalker, G.M., *The Management of Innovation* (Tavistock Publications, London, 1961).
6 Lawrence, P.R. and Lorsch, J.W., *Organisation and Environment* (Harvard Business School Press, Boston, 1986).
7 Morse, J.J. and Lorsch, J.W., 'Beyond Theory Y', *Harvard Business Review*, 48 (1970), pp. 61–8.
8 This idea is developed in Hamel, G. and Prahalad, C.K., 'Strategic intent', *Harvard Business Review*, May/June (1989), pp. 63–76.
9 Porter, M. E., 'From competitive advantage to corporate strategy', *Harvard Business Review*, 45 (1987), pp. 46–9.

ECM Unit Five

Decline and Recovery

Learning Objectives

After completing this unit you should be able to:

- understand the causes of business failure;
- use the Seven S Framework in a recovery situation;
- use the TPF concept to plan the recovery of your organization;
- understand and be able to implement the various approaches to recovery;
- apply the generic skills.

Contents

ECM Unit Five

> ❝ What should I say?
> He is so plaguey proud that the death-tokens of it
> Cry 'No recovery'.❞
>
> *Ulysses in* Troilus and Cressida[1]

A. Overview

This unit deals with the decline and possible demise of organizations, as well as with possible policies and techniques to arrest that decline.

Business failure is tackled in the first section, with indicators and manifestations of decline being combined with its typical causes. A lack of competitiveness, poor financial management and inadequate skill levels of management are seen to be important causes of failure.

The Seven S Framework is applied in an attempt to halt the rot and to recover from the malaise. Control systems and managerial style are seen to be important 'Ss' in this context. The TPF Perspective consolidates the application of the Seven S technique.

Policy or strategic options are examined in an attempt to stabilize the organization, build up its change capacity and, to a lesser extent in reality, boost enterprise. Indeed, we argue that short-term cost cutting is not sufficient. As in a football game, if you concede six goals but score seven you still win. So increased profitability through increased sales and sales turnover or whatever, rather than cost cutting, is seen as the longer-term answer to a turnaround situation. Of course, we accept that in the short term if costs are not reduced, there may be no business to turn around.

We conclude this unit by examining specific recovery scenarios, which in turn bring us on to sustaining real growth, the subject matter of Unit Six.

B. Introduction: Decline and Fall

Crisis or failure is not a unique or unexpected occurrence in business. There is a continuum in the severity of a crisis which may require a recovery to be started. At one end is the immediate prospect of insolvency and bankruptcy, while at the other is a dissatisfaction with current performance and a feeling that a recovery must be started in order to avoid more unsatisfactory results in the future.

We shall examine recovery positions later, but first we concentrate on the decline if not the death of the organization. Please refer to Box ECM5.1 and tackle Activity ECM5.1 Then read Box ECM5.2.

BOX ECM5.1

Collapse?

There are **symptoms of decline** that indicate that a business may be heading for trouble. Argenti analysed forty UK businesses which were in decline and found ten major symptoms:

1 falling profitability
2 reduced dividends
3 falling sales
4 increased debt
5 decreasing liquidity
6 delays in publishing financial results
7 reduced market share
8 high turnover of management
9 fear
10 lack of clear direction

Source:
Argenti, J., *Corporate Collapse* (McGraw-Hill, New York, 1976).

ACTIVITY ECM5.1

FAILURE

Activity code
☑ Self-development
☑ Teamwork
☑ Communications
☑ Numeracy/IT
☑ Decisions

Task

Before reading Box ECM5.2, you (or your group) should consider the main causes of business failure.

Please use three headings and derive typical examples/instances of such business failure.

The three headings are:

1 management skills
2 financial management
3 competitiveness.

BOX ECM5.2

Causes of business failure

What causes a business to fail? The causal factors may be classified under three headings, management skills, financial management and competitiveness, according to Slatter.

Management skills
- The business may be dominated by one person whose objectives or style create problems and lead to poor performance.
- New strategies, products or services may not be developed quickly enough as current ones go into decline.
- Weak managers may support the dominant leader or weak non-executive directors may allow tunnel vision to occur.
- Key issues may be ignored if managers are too functionally oriented. Businesses dominated by accountants or engineers may not pay sufficient attention to the market.
- A business undergoing rapid change of diversification may ignore its core business.
- Acquisitions may fail to meet expectations and may have cost too much in the first place.
- Large projects may be badly managed due to:
  - underestimating capital requirements;
  - design changes during production;
  - development time being longer than intended;
  - start-up difficulties not having been foreseen;
  - market entry being more expensive than expected.

Financial management
- There may be poor financial control, indicated by poor cash flow and overtrading.
- Poor costing systems may not differentiate between the products and services provided, so that if the mix changes a loss can occur.
- High fixed costs may make the business volume-sensitive.
- There may be poor budgets and a lack of attention to what the variances are telling managers.
- Lack of economies of scale and experience may give cost disadvantages.
- The business structure and product variety may give both advantages and disadvantages. For example, the overhead costs of an expensive head office may disadvantage a large business against a small one.
- Costs may be increased due to poor operating management.
- The debt ratio may not be used carefully enough so that in times of low profit the business can still invest for the future. Conservatism may lead to cash reserves and no loans, but no investment either.

Competitiveness
- Clear differentiation may not be maintained.
- Increased costs of reserves and fluctuations in the currency markets may cause problems.

- Marketing may be poor.
- Environmental forces may cause problems.

Source:
Adapted from Slatter, S., *Corporate Recovery: successful turnaround strategies and their implementation* (Penguin, London, 1984).

The causes of a decline in a business may be due to a number of factors which are interlinked. For example, a business, losing sales and therefore suffering a reduction in profits, may have high costs or lack differentiation of its products from its competitors. This could be due to poor managers who fail to control costs or create sustainable competitive advantage; or it could be due to external competitive forces which are not under management control.

Managers have to be able to distinguish the symptoms of a decline from the underlying causes. Both need attention and action. In the example above, the reduction in sales and profits may be symptoms but the causes could be the fault of management or the external environment or both.

Slatter[2] found that organizations which had many causes of decline – a severe crisis; unfavourable stakeholder attitudes; constraints from historical strategy; unfavourable industry characteristics and/or an unfavourable cost/price structure – were unlikely to be recoverable. On the other hand, enterprises which had few causes of decline – mild or no crisis; favourable stakeholder attitudes; a historical strategy that was not a constraint; favourable industry characteristics and a favourable cost/price structure – were recoverable.

Please read Box ECM5.3 to find out how London Underground dealt with a threat to their investment programme, then complete Activities ECM5.2 and ECM5.3.

BOX ECM5.3

London Underground recovers from government cuts

The London Underground has been grossly underfunded for decades. Essential work on the track, power supplies, structures, drainage, maintenance, communications and signalling has all been skimped. Much of the rolling stock is well past the end of its design life and too many stations have fallen into a state of dilapidation which a coat of paint cannot disguise. The Monopolies and Mergers Commission published exhaustive studies of London Underground at the government's request. These all confirmed the need for the continuity of investment spending at significantly higher levels than those achieved in the recent past, for at least the rest of the decade. This would mean spending over £700 million per year to provide a modern metro by the year 2007.

The Autumn Statement of 1992 dealt London Underground a savage blow. Projected levels of investment in 1993/4 were slashed by 20 per cent. Pleas that belt tightening was necessary in the face of a rise in the public sector borrowing requirement rang hollowly in the ears of public transport users, because the government expenditure on roads was planned to show a real growth of 5 per cent during the same period.

These cuts in government spending had a profound effect on London Underground's ability to provide a decent metro service by the year 2007. Most affected was the Northern Line, which was renamed the 'Misery Line' by customers. Due to the cuts in government spending, London Underground was forced to look elsewhere for funding. Derby trainmaker ABB offered a £500 million deal to supply a hundred new trains for the Northern Line, to be paid for over the next twenty years, However, such a deal needed the government's permission.

This private financing initiative gave London Underground an opportunity to acquire additional money for the projects which had been deferred time after time. London Underground evaluated this offer, as it was seen as a new way of providing new trains for its customers. The government was reluctant to give approval to lease trains since it believed the public would view this as back-door privatization. Government rules for lease deals to public-sector bodies involves the private-sector partner in sharing the financial risk. In this case, ABB would have had to undertake maintenance as well.

In order to gain government permission to lease rolling stock in this way, London Underground had to influence its key stakeholders: the government, its customers and its employees.

London Underground influenced the government through lobbying MPs and the chief executives of the boroughs served by London Underground. At the same time, strategic information was leaked to newspapers such as London's *Evening Standard* with the objective of gaining public support.

In fact the *Evening Standard* conducted a campaign championing the poor commuter, which attracted the wrath of Jimmy Knapp, leader of the largest rail union, RMT. He believed that the clauses in the contract giving the maintenance work to ABB would mean pay cuts and the loss of hundreds of jobs in the London area. The *Evening Standard* believed that the thoroughly modern metro envisaged would provide more long-term jobs for his members, cause more people to travel and boost life and business in London.

For the first time London Underground was able to win the support of the London Regional Passengers Committee (LRPC). A series of meetings was held to brief the LRPC about the potential benefits leasing would bring to customers. The LRPC then submitted a report to the government supporting the lease approach.

All employees who were to be affected by the deal were briefed on what the impact of leasing would be on their jobs, and trade union representatives were consulted. The impact on jobs was expected to be small since the changes would be phased in.

After weeks of controversy the government cleared the way for the leasing deal to provide new trains for the 'Misery Line'.

ACTIVITY ECM5.2

NON-PERFORMANCE

Activity code
- ☑ Self-development
- ☐ Teamwork
- ☐ Communications
- ☐ Numeracy/IT
- ☑ Decisions

Tasks

1 Identify the areas in which 'your' project or actual work organization or college is not performing as well as it might do.
2 Why is it not performing well? What are the symptoms? What are the causes?

ACTIVITY ECM5.3

DECLINE AND THE SEVEN S ANALYSIS

Activity code
- ☑ Self-development
- ☑ Teamwork
- ☑ Communications
- ☐ Numeracy/IT
- ☑ Decisions

Task

Using your own or group knowledge of decline and of the Seven S technique, outline a possible checklist of decline.

C. Recovery

Decline is all around. It may emanate from one or more factors, such as government laws or tariffs, changing social trends or consumer needs, or technological advances by others. Economically your organization may not be keeping up, competition may be rife, substitutes may exist or cheaper alternatives may be flooding the market. On the other hand, demand may be down altogether.

The organization's normal reaction to this is that of hard-nosed management with inadequate strategy. Cuts in staffing result in poor morale, a fetish develops about costs, while profits slip even further. There is an inward-looking mentality and a lack of real enterprise within the organization. Yet the example of Aston Martin provides a refreshing change. Before we go on to the Seven S analysis, please refer to Box ECM5.4.

BOX ECM5.4

Recovery at Aston Martin

When Ford bought Aston Martin in 1987 it seemed more than likely that another piece of British motoring racing history might disappear.[1] This transaction began when Walter Hayes, a retired Ford executive on a visit to Europe, learned that Aston Martin, a famous sports car of the post-war years when owned by Sir David Brown, was for sale. In fact Aston Martin had been teetering between debt and bankruptcy for years. Hayes went back to America and persuaded Henry Ford II to buy Aston Martin just twenty-eight days before his death.

Hayes was persuaded by Ford to return from retirement to head Aston Martin. Ford provided the manufacturing knowhow and Nick Fry, a young sales and manufacturing expert who had headed teams working on the Fiesta and Mondeo. His first job was to iron out the faults and inefficiencies of the 'V' cars – the Virage and Vantage coupés and the Volante convertible. The cars were hand built using jigs and often quite small pieces of aluminium. The quaint factory at Newport Pagnell was so outdated that body shells had to be pushed on little carts across the main road for painting and then back again to have engines and interiors fitted. Production there had to be streamlined.

It was also clear that production of about a hundred cars per year that sold for more than £130,000 each left the business wide open to the vagaries of fashion and the economy.

Hayes understood what the name of Aston Martin meant and returned to the principles of the period when Aston Martin was most successful. Therefore, he set about raiding the Ford empire for ideas in order to find a way to build the Aston Martin of the future, the DB7. This had to be a smaller, lighter car. He found the floor pan at Jaguar, Ford's other English acquisition. Jaguar had scrapped its project to build an F-type sports car. This and the straight six-cylinder engine became the basis for the new DB7. The new car was produced at the Bloxham plant near Banbury, where the limited run of the XJ220 supercar had been built. The result is 'a blisteringly beautiful car with a performance that could knock the red skin off a Ferrari'.

In two years Hayes achieved the impossible. He persuaded Ford to part with millions of pounds to develop and assemble a supercar. The DB7 has virtually sold out the first year's production and is now getting ready to increase production from 600 to 800 cars per year.

Hays has now retired again but has left a team with the enthusiasm and dedication to re-establish Aston Martin as a desirable car around the world; put Aston Martin back on the race track; and produced a range of cars that reaches the height of sophistication.

In four years' time that range will change again when the 'V' cars effectively reach the end of their lives. Newport Pagnell will then become the centre for a new Lagonda. By that time Aston Martin will be making 1,200 cars per year – just enough to keep demand high and ensure exclusivity.

Source:
1 Adapted from Eason, K., 'Cars that dreams are made of', *The Times*, 29 October (1994).

Now we shall use the Seven S Framework as a mechanism to analyse how an organization could react in a recovery situation.

The Seven S Framework

Strategy
The existing strategy is not working. From all that has gone before it is obvious that there is a need to carry out one or more of the following:

- change or re-emphasize the chosen generic strategy of either focus, differentiation or low cost to rebuild the market position;
- change the value chain to support the generic strategy;
- merge with another enterprise and develop synergy;
- return to a core of products and customers which are closely aligned with the strengths of the enterprise.

The detailed analysis indicated in earlier units is crucial before embarking on any of the paths suggested above.

Structure
This should follow the strategy and therefore needs to change also. The firm may need to be reorganized and the concepts of centralization and decentralization will need to be examined. Associated with these are the concepts of responsibility and control. Which of these are relevant to your organization at this time?

Systems
Invariably, when an enterprise is in a recovery situation the focus is on financial performance. New financial controls can be expected to be imposed together with the restructuring of debts. However, there are many

different systems involved in running an organization, such as capital budgeting, training, accounting, management information, communication, information, planning and business systems. All of these must be examined to see if they should be improved in any way.

The value chain described in Unit Three is seen here as the key to deciding the systems required in a business. This is because the value chain identifies the key activities both inside and outside the business which are essential to its success. Indeed, according to Porter[3] the value chain itself must be managed as a system rather than as a collection of separate activities.

To control any part of the value chain, managers need information. Therefore, the information system is the key to the development and control of a business. Information systems are now almost indispensable for planning, decision making and controlling a business. The speed and accuracy of the information about what is going right or wrong in a business determines its performance. Therefore managers have to be comfortable with computers at all levels of management.

Management information represents the key features of a situation which requires action. It should be accurate, relevant and timely. The information has to be developed from raw data and put into a form which managers can use to make decisions. Data is a collection of unorganized facts, opinions, statistics or predictions. When data means something to someone so that it can be used for decision making, it becomes information. In order to be used as information, data should be accurate, available, comprehensive, consistent, relevant, reliable, timely and useful.

Information systems provide major benefits by:

- allowing routine tasks, such as stock control and recording transactions, to be performed faster or more cheaply;
- helping people in business make better decisions;
- improving customer service;
- improving old or creating new products;
- changing the basis of competition;
- adapting quickly to change, taking advantage of short product life cycles and exploring niche markets.

There are five general areas where control is required, particularly in a recovery situation: finance, organization/people, production, quality and stock:

1 **Financial control** is carried out using budgets, analysis of the accounting statements and ratio analysis.
2 **Organization/people control** includes the organization structure and its planning and decision-making systems, together with the control of employees.
3 **Production control** is the routing, scheduling, and timing of a product, service or project.

4 **Quality control** maintains the quality of products or services.

5 **Stock control** is focused on raw materials, work in progress, finished goods and warehousing.

In a recovery situation, many controls which should increase motivation are very often threatening to employees. Therefore, the goals of the business and the objectives on which the standards are based should be explained to employees. Employees who develop the necessary standards also have a commitment to meeting the controls. The standards should be relevant and appropriate. Therefore, the clear communication of goals and standards, realistic appraisal, timely feedback and employee participation create confidence in the control system.

If employees believe the standards are more important than the business objectives on which they are based, then **goal displacement** occurs. For example, emphasis on profits can decrease long-term investment and damage the future of the business.

Overcontrol can lead to sub-optimal results. For example, reducing costs in one part of the value chain may increase costs in another, and even increase the total costs. Therefore consideration of the value chain is important at all times.

Overcontrol can also be used to gain power and may lead to higher costs, increased labour turnover, low morale and reduced production.

Management control systems guide and motivate managers to attain the business goals and to correct ineffective and inefficient performance. In order to stimulate recovery, the management control process should have the following features:

- It should focus both on activities to achieve goals and on responsibility centres. An activity such as a product line may involve several responsibility centres.

- The process should involve two types of information: planned data (budgets and standards) and actual data (what has actually happened in a business or externally).

- The process should co-ordinate and optimize all parts of a business, and therefore has to be an integrated system.

- It should tend to focus on financial controls.

- The process should involve periodic planning and feedback.

The management control system includes both formal and informal controls. The informal controls are just as important and form part of the business culture.

The overall goals of a business tend to be timeless and set the overall guidelines for the management control. In turn, management control sets the guidelines for task control.

Management control generally controls people and is used to control the whole business. It ensures that the business achieves its goals. **Task control**, on the other hand, ensures that tasks are completed efficiently and effectively and are designed specifically for a particular task. It generally controls things and is more precise than management control in that it is based on a set of rules and procedures and normally provides exact numerical standards for evaluating performance.

If a system is a set of interrelated parts or a structure that functions as one unit, then a management control system is based on the parts of the business – its structure – and the information flows between the parts. The process is what the managers do with the information.

Controls ensure desired results are obtained. First managers should determine the **key activities** which must function effectively for the business to be successful. At the same time it is important to identify **key control points** where monitoring and collecting information should occur. These are usually at points of change. Please tackle Activity ECM5.4.

ACTIVITY ECM5.4

CONTROL

Activity code
- ✓ Self-development
- ✓ Teamwork
- ✓ Communications
- ✓ Numeracy/IT
- ✓ Decisions

Tasks

With reference to 'your' organization or college, or to one which you know well, discuss the following:

1 the five general areas where control is required;
2 the concepts of management control and task control;
3 the key activities which must function effectively for the business to be successful;
4 the key control points where the monitoring and collection of information should occur.

Style

Changes in the top management and the chief executive officer are often needed, since a special type of leadership is required in a recovery situation. Management needs to be directive, tough and innovative. At the same time, attention must also be paid to improving morale and motivation.

Staff

Human resources are of paramount importance in a recovery situation. Both the management and the workforce may need to be reduced drastically, and ways for doing this with sensitivity have to be explored. Training and development may have to be increased and incentives developed. New methods of working may need to be developed, such as teamwork and quality circles or the Japanese concept of *kaizen* (continuous improvement).

Skills

As was mentioned in the section above on 'strategy', the value chain has to be examined in a search for ways to increase efficiency and reduce costs. Please see Boxes ECM5.5 and ECM5.6.

BOX ECM5.5

Recovery at Hewlett-Packard

In 1985, a computer product division of Hewlett-Packard found that a new product failed to meet its market share and contribution targets because the overhead allocation was too high. They found that as the product passed through the manufacturing process it was absorbing costs that it did not incur. This discovery led to the use of activity-based costing (ABC), which is founded on the fact that products consume activities and activities consume resources.

Activity-based costing
The normal costing system assigns overhead costs to the final product, whereas ABC identifies the costs of the activities involved in the production process. Costs are collected for each activity and so final product costs are built up from the sum of the costs of the preceding activities. The aim is to reduce low-value-added overheads and so cost and price products and services more effectively.

Johnson reports that one General Electric plant achieved a 60 per cent reduction in product lead time, a 50 per cent reduction in product defects, a 21 per cent reduction in total payroll cost per unit, and a 50 per cent cut in work in progress after nine months of changes based on ABC.

Since it is extremely difficult to change manufacturing costs of products after their launch, **cost drivers** are a vital influence on design engineering decisions. This leads to the concept of **design for manufacturability**, which is based on ABC.

The success of ABC in Hewlett-Packard owed much to the decisions to:
- use a team of manufacturing, R & D and accounting representatives to identify the processes to be monitored and the cost drivers to be used;
- start with a few cost drivers in order to master the techniques and reports.

Hewlett-Packard later found that ABC could be extended from manufacture to other functions in the business. They became heavily committed to **continuous process improvement**, which is the elimination of waste and the refining of processes, methods and movements so that 'cycle times' and 'time to market' are optimized.

Although many people accept that most organizations have a minimum of 30 per cent waste in the cost structure, accountants have not seen waste as a major source of profit improvement. They would rather use downsizing, reducing costs by 10 per cent, stopping all recruitment or capital projects. In 1992, Hewlett-Packard was a $16-billion company spending $8 billion in expenses. If the 30 per cent wastage figure is correct, then there was a $2.4-billion opportunity for profit improvement. Is that not worth chasing when compared with the paltry amounts produced by downsizing and other techniques usually introduced by accountants and managers?

Process management

Everything a business does is part of a process, but managers still plan, monitor and control their businesses on a functional or departmental basis. They analyse and measure the type of expense rather than why the money is spent and on what business process.

The functional managers in the Hewlett-Packard division identified their six key business processes as shown in the diagram below.

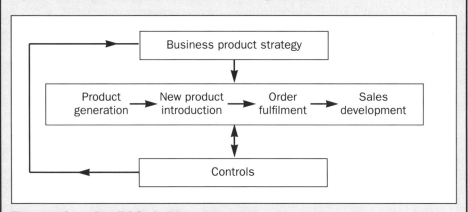

The manufacturing division's key processes

A **process matrix** was developed by interviewing each department. The managers had to provide annual budgets, their asset base and a human resources plan. They also had to think through the tasks and activities undertaken and the key processes that initiated or benefited from the work done. To ease understanding, figures were rounded up. In this way the functional cost structure was reformed into the process matrix shown overleaf.

Key process	Mfg	R & D	Mktg	Admin.	Totals
Business product strategy Product generation New product introduction Order fulfilment Sales development Control					
Totals					

The process matrix

Two benefits quickly developed out of this exercise:

1 There was a gut reaction to the costs of the activities which questioned their values – 'If that's what it costs then I don't need it.'
2 The importance of links between the departments was recognized and there was a focus on who the customer was and whether the product or service met the needs.

These developments were followed up by an effort to quantify the **process cost indicators**, particularly the **non-value-added** element in each activity or process. This identified waste, duplication or inefficiency and the owners for each process (see the chart below).

Process	Owner	Total costs (£1000s)	Value added (%)	Non-value-added (%)
Business product generation	General manager			
Product generation	R & D			
New product introduction	Mktg			
Order fulfilment	Mfg			
Sales development	Mktg			
Control	Admin.			

Process cost indicators

Hewlett-Packard were surprised to find that the manufacturing element of the order fulfilment process was the most efficient and their precious resources of R & D and marketing were the most wasteful. However, in view of these results Hewlett-Packard did not cut their budgets to improve the bottom line, but set about improving their 'time to market' and developing products to get higher sales growth in order to generate the profits.

The results of this exercise stimulated Hewlett-Packard to think about restructuring their organization from a functional focus into empowered process teams. These were to be cross-functional so that process and performance improvements could be continuously generated and implemented.

To summarize:

- Activity-based costing indicates where the opportunities exist.
- Process management directs and influences the priorities for improvement.

Sources:
Adapted from Rigby, J., 'Activity based costing and process re-engineering at Hewlett-Packard', in *Successful Change Strategies*, ed. B. Taylor (Institute of Directors, London, 1994); and Johnson, H.T., 'Performance measurements for competitive excellence', in *Measures for Manufacturing Excellence*, ed. R.S. Kaplan (Harvard Business School Press, Boston, 1990).

BOX ECM5.6

Recovery at Rank Xerox

When the patents on which Rank Xerox based its business ran out, the competition moved in and the market share slumped. Profits started to halve year on year, and Rank Xerox were rapidly going out of business.[1] They assumed the Japanese were dumping in Europe and the USA to gain market share. The Rank Xerox response was to increase shipments and wait until the competitors pulled out.

The chief executive was not so sure and visited Japan to look at the competition more closely. He found that Rank Xerox had nine times as many suppliers, ten times the assembly-line reject rates, double the product-to-market times, and double the indirect/direct cost ratio of competitors. This resulted in competitors being able to sell equivalent products with 100 per cent profit margin but still at a price that was less than the Rank Xerox manufacturing cost. Obviously the strategy of riding out the storm was doomed to failure.

However, his senior managers would not believe him until a deputation went to Japan to see for themselves. Since then Rank Xerox have tried to involve people in all their fact finding and analysis – employee involvement.

Process management
In 1980 the first of a number of quality programmes began. These had limited success, but Rank Xerox learned from the work done, so that by 1987 customer satisfaction was a top priority for them. They began to:

- expect all employees to be involved in improving their work processes, which was to produce a 10–20 per cent increase in efficiency (*Business as usual*);
- look for improvements to be made to cross-functional processes and so produce a 100 per cent increase in efficiency (*Simplification*).
- develop a vision-led approach to key processes to produce a 1,000 per cent increase in efficiency (*Process re-engineering*).

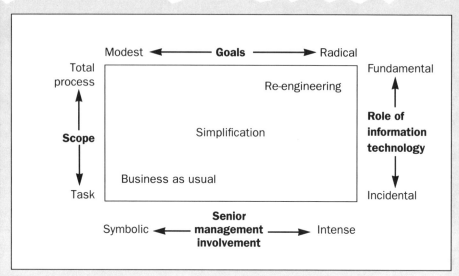

Process management

This is shown in the diagram above.

Over the years, Rank Xerox found that crucial processes which deliver value to the customer operate across internal functional boundaries. There was no manager who owned the total process, since they were organized by functions. Improving the functions produced some benefits but not enough, since functional specialization was letting them down. The plan was to introduce process owners at board level so that a director was responsible for the process regardless of the functions involved in it.

A map of all the key processes and their interactions has been developed and process owners at different levels assigned. Full process management is on the way.

Rank Xerox have developed a model for business excellence based on all the development work which they have undertaken (see the diagram below).

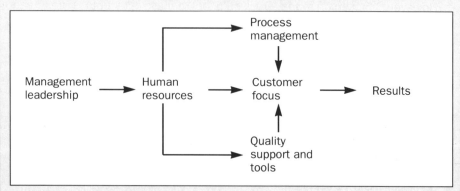

A model for business excellence

This model, with the customer at its centre, is used to prioritize work in the organization. Management leadership focuses human resources on the customer. The focus on customers is driven by process management, which is improved by quality support and tools. The achievement of business objectives and good results should follow.

Pearson finds it interesting to compare this model with the classical approach, in which, when profits fall, companies begin to cut costs. This usually means cutting human resources, which leads to less focus on the customer, which in turn leads to a drop in profits or results – a downward spiral.

If your results are not good, then, using the business excellence model, you examine the customer focus and work back through the model. In this way the corrections made address the root cause and do not simplistically reduce costs.

This model is used for the Rank Xerox self-assessment process. Each of the six elements is divided into its major components; for instance, human resources is divided into recruitment, education and development, compensation, etc. For each element a desired state is defined. The desired state is that of the benchmark organization in that particular area.

Every assessment is made against the benchmark, using a combination of results (hard measures showing a trend towards the goals), processes (with a link between processes and results) and pervasiveness (whether all the necessary people are involved).

Year-on-year improvements are expected. External examiners are brought in to check the self-assessment is accurate and to provide consistency across the company. The results are published internally so that best practice can be shared. The results are also used as a basis for the planning process, since the strengths and weaknesses in the organization provide the key to further development.

Source:

1 Adapted from Pearson, G., 'Increasing profit and market share through total quality management', *Successful Change Strategies*, ed. B. Taylor (Institute of Directors, 1994).

Shared values

A recovery situation very often requires a change in attitudes and values in both the workforce and management, which may affect the whole culture of the enterprise.

The TPF Perspective

Please consolidate the recovery position by examining Activity ECM5.5.

ACTIVITY ECM5.5

TPF: A RECOVERY STRATEGY

Activity code
- ✓ Self-development
- ✓ Teamwork
- ✓ Communications
- ✓ Numeracy/IT
- ✓ Decisions

Task

Using the TPF Perspective, identify the key areas on which you (or your group) would expect that senior management should focus their attention in a situation of recovery.

D. Change and Enterprise Management

Since the organization is in a critical condition, any change is liable to destabilize it even further. On the other hand, not to change at all will invite disaster, and growth is impossible. Therefore, there must be a decision to stop the decline in order to start a recovery. We propose an imposed change with a vision of enterprise.

Approaches to recovery

According to Jauch and Glueck,[4] there are four major approaches to recovery:

1. reducing costs
2. increasing revenues
3. reducing assets
4. reorganizing products and/or markets to achieve greater efficiency.

Reducing costs

Cost cutting is best when the enterprise is close to break-even, when radical surgery is possible and operating inefficiencies can be identified and corrected. Alongside cost cutting, budgets need to be examined, jobs need cutting, and plant and equipment need modernizing to gain greater production efficiency. You must also delay any non-essential capital expenses but be aware of the long-term consequence of such moves. We believe this to be a short-term 'solution', for encouraging enterprise will make the sick patient well again.

Key cost areas are administration, production and sales costs. Managers tend to focus on human resources (which have the most dramatic effect), materials and parts of the enterprise which do not have much impact on the turnover in the short term (R & D, training, public relations and advertising, and general overheads such as staff, fringe benefits, consumables, etc.). Managers should be aware that cost reduction activities can damage the organization's image.

Increasing revenues

This is necessary when:

- it is not possible to cut costs further and still break even;
- full utilization of existing capacity is the key to profitability.

There are various ways to stimulate sales: incentives for sales staff and distributors, changes to products, a new marketing strategy, price cuts, increased promotion, a bigger sales force, added customer services, etc. If buyer demand is not price sensitive, price cuts will not build volume, so a price rise should be considered.

Reducing assets

This is essential when cash flow is critical and when the most practical ways to generate cash are as follows:

- The sale of assets in terms of subsidiaries, stock, patents, land, plant, equipment, etc. Divestment of businesses, particularly loss makers, may be at less than asset value. On the other hand, selling profit makers will provide cash flow but may affect the long-term health of the enterprise.
- Cutting marginal products from the product line, closing or selling old plant, reducing workforce, withdrawing from distant markets, cutting back on customer service, etc.
- Sell and leaseback.
- Reduction in stock and work in progress. This reduces the asset base and releases cash.
- Reducing debtors and increasing the length of time you take to pay creditors. This also releases cash. Some creditors may have to co-operate, since if they were to insist on payment it could result in liquidation of your enterprise and only a small amount of their debt being repaid.

Reorganizing products and/or markets

This approach can include dropping some products or markets to achieve efficiency, or vertically integrating the organization. Essentially these approaches reverse the flow implied in figure ECM4.4 (Unit Four). Managers should look for defensible segments of the market and redefine the business.

If sales are 15–20 per cent of the industry leader's, then the chances of survival should be good if you concentrate on the markets where your strengths are greatest and deploy your assets accordingly. If sales are a small percentage of the industry leader's, then concentrate on a defensible niche market where you have or can develop a competitive advantage. You may have to reduce your asset base to fund the necessary R & D and marketing.

Successful low-share businesses can be expected to have high-quality, medium-price products. They will spend carefully on marketing and R & D and sometimes develop vertical integration in order to reduce costs and control quality.

In a declining market, the objective should be to concentrate on those market segments which will not die. Most competitors will tend to resist decline throughout the market rather than identify the segments which will survive.

In difficult situations, it is often necessary to use several of these approaches at the same time. However, Hall[5] found no successful recoveries among the most troubled companies in the eight basic industries he studied: the recovery attempt was too late. This emphasizes the need to monitor your enterprise and its environment continuously and be sensitive to the signals noticed. Remember: a manager must be looking for continuous improvement in performance and not be satisfied with the current situation.

Please read Box ECM5.7 and then Box ECM5.8.

BOX ECM5.7

The Z Factor

Altman developed a useful predictor for the bankruptcy of manufacturing businesses. He uses the **Z Factor**, which is a discriminant function with five significant ratios:

$$Z = 1.2A + 1.4B + 3.3C + 0.6D + E$$

where:

A = Working capital/Total assets
B = Retained earnings/Total assets
C = Earnings before interest and tax/Total assets
D = Market value of equity/Book value of total debt
E = Sales/Total assets

and where:

- Working capital   = Current assets – Current liabilities
- Total assets   = Fixed assets + Current assets
- Retained earnings   = Accumulated profits

- Market value of equity = (Number of ordinary shares × Current market price) + Value of preference shares
- Book value of total debt = Long-term + Medium-term + Short-term loans + Overdraft

For Z Factors in the UK, if the Z value is less than 1.5 then businesses are fairly sure to go bankrupt, whereas businesses with a Z Factor or more than 2.0 are almost certain not to.

Z Factors between 1.5 and 2.0 give cause for concern if repeated over several periods.

In order to compare businesses, it is best to use the Z Factor for businesses in the same industry and phase of the organization life cycle.

Source:
Adapted from Altman, E.I., 'Financial ratios, discriminant analysis and the prediction of corporate bankruptcy', *Journal of Finance*, 23(4), (1968).

BOX ECM5.8

Good housekeeping or relative decline?

Some organizations have favoured a policy of cost cutting in order to remain competitive. Hoover's retreat to Scotland from France to utilize cheap(er) labour can be cited as an example. Similarly, the Vespa scooter manufacturer Piaggio's planned development of the Mezzogiorno, south of Naples, with potential state aid, can also be seen as a move to cut costs. Thus both companies have taken steps to reduce costs – particularly labour costs – in Dijon and Pontedera respectively, by reducing labour charges through cheap(er) labour.

Costs must be contained for business efficiency, but we cannot help feeling that sometimes this moving or trimming back of labour is almost an end in itself.

The ways in which enterprises can survive and prosper in hostile environments are indicated in Box ECM5.9. When you have read it, please tackle Activity ECM5.6.

BOX ECM5.9

Survival strategies in a hostile environment

Hall reported the preliminary findings of a research study that showed that success is possible even in a hostile environment.[1] He found that in the basic industries studied, the industry leaders earned a return on equity in the top 20 per cent of the *Fortune* '1,000' industrials list. The average returns for the sample of eight industries on both return on equity and return on capital were ahead of the leading oil company, technology leaders, progressive diversifiers and acquisition experts at the time. They also grew faster than most leading companies.

Hall was able to show that survival and prosperity are possible even in a hostile environment and when industry trends become unfavourable. A hostile environment could offer an excellent investment climate for opportunity and reinvestment. The usual advice to competitors in basic industries to diversify, divest or accept below-average returns was not correct.

The strategies which led to success had common characteristics irrespective of the industries studied. The firms had a single-minded determination to achieve one or both of the following competitive positions:

1 Achieve the lowest delivered cost relative to the competition coupled with acceptable delivered quality and a pricing policy to gain profitable volume and market-share growth.

   The lowest cost leader grows slowly, holding down price increases and operating margins to gain volume, fixed-cost reductions and improved asset turnover. Such competitors also have lower sales turnover than differentiated producers, which reflect the higher asset investment needed to gain cost reductions in production and distribution.

2 Achieve the highest product, service or quality differentiated position relative to the competition, coupled with an acceptable delivered-cost structure and pricing policy, to gain margins sufficient to fund investment in product or service differentiation.

   The differentiated leader grows faster, with higher prices and operating margins to cover promotion, R & D and other product or service costs. Such competitors operate with higher sales turnover and lower asset investments, which reflect both the higher prices they can charge and the lower cost asset base.

Successful businesses strove for a leadership position. This consistency and clarity of purpose helped to mobilize and co-ordinate internal resources in order to gain and defend a leadership position.

The time-phased pattern of investment decisions was based on 'doing the right things' to gain leadership in lower costs and/or differentiation. All the high performers used careful strategic analysis to guide their investments, not simplistic tools like share/growth matrices, experience curves or PIMS.

Leaders in mature markets were not milked but aggressively re-invested in. Diversification was not considered. Low-cost production was not essential in mature markets, contrary to the views of those who believe in the experience curve. High sustainable returns came from re-investing in an average-cost, highly differentiated position.

High market share and long experience are not essential for cost leadership in a mature market as indicated by the experience curve and the profit impact of market strategy (PIMS). For example, firms have focused on modern, automated-process technology and invested heavily in their distribution system to gain economies of scale and other cost reductions in the value chain.

Vertical integration is not necessary to exploit cost leadership in mature markets. Instead, industry leaders invested to have the most efficient technology in at least one stage of the value chain.

Hall found that problems came from failing to gain or defend a leadership position. Much depended on the reinvestment decisions, and Hall gives examples of leading firms which made the wrong decisions.

For young mature firms in hostile environments, diversification is not always a good recovery approach. Most firms lack the capital and management skills to enter new markets and/or grow such businesses successfully. Management commitment and a focus on the core business to provide a steady flow of capital for investment will ensure growth and vitality.

Source:

1 Adapted from Hall, W.K. 'Survival strategies in a hostile environment', *Harvard Business Review*, 58 (1980), pp. 75–85.

ACTIVITY ECM5.6

AN ACTION PLAN FOR RECOVERY

Activity code

- ☑ Self-development
- ☐ Teamwork
- ☑ Communications
- ☑ Numeracy/IT
- ☑ Decisions

Tasks

1 In Activity ECM5.2 you identified the causes of decline in the performance of 'your' organization or college. Explain the various ways in which you can go about recovering the situation.

2 Outline a plan of action for recovery.

E. Fine-tuning Recovery

There are a number of tasks which will help you to fine-tune recovery situations:

- Set up an information system which will indicate when a crisis is developing.
- Continuously monitor costs and look for ways of reducing them.
- Examine the asset base – is it too large for the sales and profits being generated? Is it obsolete?
- Examine whether you can increase revenue by changing prices, finding new markets, better marketing, quality, etc.
- Top management may not be suitable for the current and/or future environment. If you are a top manager, when do/should you decide to go? Can you change, and can you change your enterprise? What evidence have you got for saying yes?

Now we have a series of activities (Activities ECM5.7–5.9) with suggested solutions in boxes (Boxes ECM5.10–5.12), covering organizations coming to terms with change and enterprise in mature and fragmented industries and in low-market-share types of business.

ACTIVITY ECM5.7

MATURE BUT NOT SENILE

Activity code
☑ Self-development
☐ Teamwork
☐ Communications
☐ Numeracy/IT
☑ Decisions

Task

The industry is stagnant, so which generic strategy should you follow?

BOX ECM5.10

The mature or declining industry

In response to Activity ECM 5.7: an enterprise in a mature or declining industry is often struggling for survival since demand is either growing very slowly or declining. Hamermesh and Silk found that the companies that succeeded in stagnant industries relied on one of Porter's generic strategies.[1]

- They identified, created and exploited the growth segments in the industry – focused on a niche. Slow-growth and declining industries have many segments, one or two of which continue to grow relative to the industry as a whole.
- They differentiated their products/services using quality and innovation. This created new growth segments and induced buyers to trade up. Innovation can be difficult for rivals to imitate.
- Since increased sales could not be expected to increase earnings, they drove costs down by reducing operating costs and increasing efficiency. For example, they automated the product process and increased specialization; consolidated underutilized facilities; increased distribution channels; closed low-volume, high-cost outlets; and examined the value chain to eliminate some cost-producing tasks.

Do not get trapped into a war of attrition, divert money out of the business too quickly or be complacent and hope that things will improve in the future. You must be proactive and strive for continuous improvement in performance.

Source:

1 Adapted from Hamermesh, R.G., and Silk, S.B., 'How to compete in stagnant industries', *Harvard Business Review*, 57 (1979), p. 161.

ACTIVITY ECM5.8

FRAGMENTED BUT NOT BROKEN

Activity code
- ☑ Self-development
- ☑ Teamwork
- ☑ Communications
- ☐ Numeracy/IT
- ☐ Decisions

A fragmented industry consists of hundreds, if not thousands, of small, medium and large enterprises. Many of these are privately owned but none has a large share of the total industry sales. There tends to be an absence of market leaders with the ability to set the standards for competition. For example, typical industries are hotels, restaurants and fast food, hair dressing, clothes, furniture and DIY.

Thompson and Strickland believe that an enterprise in a fragmented indus-try is in a weak position relative to Porter's five forces.[1] The bargaining posi-tion with buyers and suppliers is weak, new entrants are always a threat, sub-stitutes may or may not be a threat, and competitive rivalry may range from weak to fierce. Therefore there are many entrances into and exits from the market.

Task

By group or individual effort:

1 account for the factors making for industry fragmentation;
2 determine policies to overcome these fragmentation difficulties.

Source:

1 Thompson, A.A. and Strickland, A.J., *Strategic Management: concepts and cases* (Irwin, Holmewood, IL, 1992).

BOX ECM5.11

The fragmented industry

Several factors can account for the fragmented nature of an industry, as out-lined in Activity ECM5.8.[1]

- There are low entry barriers.
- An absence of economies of scale enables small and large enterprises to compete in the same market.
- Buyers often require small quantities of customized products, so sales volumes cannot normally support production, marketing and distribution on a scale that favours a large enterprise.
- The market is local and so favours those enterprises with local knowledge of buyers and markets.
- The industry demand is so large and diverse that it requires a large number of enterprises to satisfy it.
- High transport costs may limit the radius within which an enterprise can service its customers.
- The geographic areas are unique.
- The industry is new.

Recovery for an organization in trouble is based on developing a loyal cus-tomer base and generating sales using one of the generic strategies. Focus, differentiation and low-cost themes are all possible. For instance, you could:

- construct and operate 'formula' facilities;
- become a low-cost operator;
- increase customer value through integration;
- specialize by product/service type;
- specialize by customer type;
- focus on a limited geographic area.

This is another example of the use of Porter's five forces and three generic strategies to position an enterprise in its market.

Source:

1 Adapted from Thompson, A.A. and Strickland, A.J., *Strategic Management: concepts and cases* (Irwin, Holmewood, IL, 1992).

ACTIVITY ECM5.9

LOW MARKET SHARE

Activity code

☑ Self-development
☑ Teamwork
☑ Communications
☐ Numeracy/IT
☐ Decisions

Woo and Cooper used the PIMS SP125.DTA database to identify strategies which were effective in low-market-share businesses.[1] This work is an important contribution to knowledge since most businesses are not market leaders. The strategies identified are based on decisions taken at two levels:

1   product/market choices at corporate level;
2   competitive strategy at the business level.

Woo and Cooper believe the product/market choice defines the short-term environment of the business. This choice, made by the corporate manager, constrains the business manager, who is unable to make product/market changes in the short term. Since a market is located in an industry, some of the industry variables are also included. The variables chosen for the competitive strategy define the competitive position of the business relative to others.

Task

By group or individual effort, outline possible variables concerning product/market and industry decisions in a low-market-share company.

Source:

1 Adapted from Woo, C.Y.Y. and Cooper, A.C., 'Strategies of effective, low share businesses', *Strategic Management Journal*, 2 (1981), pp. 301–18.

BOX ECM5.12

Low-market-share businesses

In response to Activity ECM5.8: the variables on which these choices are made are indicated below:

Product/market and industry	**Competitive strategy**
Type of product	Relative price
Standardization of products	Relative quality
Importance of auxiliary services	Relative product breadth
Product life-cycle stage	Relative emphasis on new products
Purchase frequency (end user)	Proprietary products
Purchase frequency (immediate user)	Proprietary processes
Geographic location	R & D intensity (product)
Industry value-added	R & D intensity (process)
Industry concentration	Relative advertising
Number of competitors	Relative sales force
Real market growth	Relative vertical integration (backwards)
Industry growth	Relative vertical integration (forwards)
Frequency of product changes	Relative direct costs

Woo and Cooper contrasted the effective low-market-share businesses with:

- effective high-market-share businesses, because of unequal resources available;
- ineffective low-market-share businesses, because of differences in performance.

The PIMS database used has over two hundred variables describing businesses, which were defined as 'a division, product line, or other profit centre within its parent company, selling a distinct set of products or services to an identifiable group or groups of customers, in competition with a well-defined set of competitors'. The following limitations of this data were noted by Woo and Cooper:

- Most businesses in PIMS tend to be divisions of large corporations and therefore enjoy privileges and constraints which are largely absent from independent low-share businesses.
- The contributors of data to PIMS do not always apply the definition guidelines in a uniform way.
- The database cannot support time-series analyses.
- Analysis of the PIMS data is limited to the statistical package available with it.
- Foreign businesses and non-manufacturing businesses are excluded.

Conclusions

Effective low-market-share businesses were concentrated in certain product/market environments which provided them with a degree of stability because of:

- very slow real market growth and infrequent product changes;
- sale of standardized industrial components and supplies without the provision of custom features or auxiliary services;

- high purchase frequency, high value-added and large numbers of competitors.

These findings challenge the general recommendation that low-share businesses should locate in growth markets and provide special services or custom features. Such features are more characteristics of effective high-market-share businesses.

Ineffective low-market-share businesses were found in the same product/market environments, but they differed from the effective low-market-share businesses in the way they competed. The latter focused on specific strengths, intense marketing, high product value and careful cost control.

Ineffective low-market-share businesses adopted aggressive postures which paralleled the competitive strategies of effective high-market-share businesses. Both had broad product lines, engaged in R & D, assumed an intensive marketing posture and operated at higher levels of vertical integration. Ineffective low-market-share businesses did not enjoy similar returns because the scale of operation was not large enough to support all of these activities, since their resources had been spread too thinly. Hence a restricted focus on key competitive activities was necessary for low-market-share success.

Effective low-market-share businesses tended to pursue a high-quality, low-price policy complemented by limited spending on marketing, R & D and vertical integration.

Source:
Adapted from Woo, C.Y.Y. and Cooper, A.C., 'Strategies of effective low share businesses', *Strategic Management Journal*, 2 (1981), pp. 301–18.

F. A Vision of Toughness

Clearly there is a range of policy options which can be adopted to turn the business around and to arrest decline.

Perhaps change management dominates at the expense of enterprising management in these contexts of absolute and relative decline. An authoritarian style, a centralized structure, an emphasis on control systems, a lack of proactive people management (seen in a lack of skill training and shedding labour to cut out costs), allied to a dominant no-nonsense managerial value system, are seen to characterize many of these strategic options of turnaround. Perhaps a different management, one that encompasses these attributes, is needed to handle this vision of recovery. Once the recovery is under way, an enterprising vision may be beyond the scope of these turnaround managers. However, a 'softer' approach to turnaround may cement change and enterprise. Please refer to Box ECM5.13.

Then, with or without new managers or with degrees of softness and hardness, we now turn to growth and expansion in the final unit.

BOX ECM5.13

Turnaround: a 'soft' approach

Pascarella[1] argues that strategy must be 'wired in' to allow flexibility and creativity to deal with change. The key, he suggests, is not planning *per se*, but values, vision and corporate mission.

Behaviour can indeed be influenced by such attitudinal change and the most important mechanism of attitudinal structuring is through ongoing training and development. However, if we look at Long's spectrum[2] or Gagné's hierarchy of learning,[3] attitudinal change deals with 'self/social' change and 'principle/rule' learning respectively. Both are difficult to achieve.

Sources:

1 Pascarella, P., 'The toughest turnaround of all', *Industry Week*, 2 April (1984).

2 Long, C.G.L., 'A theoretical model for method selection', *Industrial Training International*, 4 (1969), pp. 475–8. These concepts are discussed in Anderson, A.H., *Successful Training Practice* (Blackwell Publishers, Oxford, 1993), chs 1 and 3.

3 Gagné, R., *The Conditions of Learning* (Holt, Rinehart and Winston, New York, 1965).

Notes

1 Shakespeare, *Troilus and Cressida*, Act II, sc.iii, 171–3.

2 Slatter, S., *Corporate Recovery: successful turnaround strategies and their implementation* (Penguin, London, 1984).

3 Porter, M.E., *Competitive Strategy: techniques for analyzing industries and competitors* (Free Press, New York, 1980).

4 Jauch, L.R. and Glueck, W.F., *Business Policy and Strategic Management* (McGraw-Hill, New York, 1988).

5 Hall, W.K., 'Survival strategies in a hostile environment', *Harvard Business Review*, 58 (1980), pp. 75–85.

ECM Unit Six

Growth

Learning Objectives

After completing this unit you should be able to:

- understand the concept of growth and its various dynamics;
- develop specific growth strategies;
- use the Seven S and the TPF techniques for analysing the dynamics of growth;
- relate growth strategies to change and enterprise;
- fine-tune the growth strategies;
- apply the generic skills.

Contents

A. Overview

B. Introduction

C. Growth

▶ The Seven S Framework

D. Change and Enterprise Management

▶ Internal expansion

▶ External expansion

E. Fine-Tuning

▶ Portfolio management

▶ The Seven S Framework

▶ The TPF Perspective

ECM Unit Six

> ❝ The ideal team at the top includes a visionary. The visionary has to be a true member of the team, but doesn't have to be the No. 1 person.❞
>
> *R. Drake*[1]

A. Overview

This unit, as its title implies, is about growth or expansion and so involves enterprise in terms of taking advantage of new opportunities and turning threats into opportunities. At the same time, growth involves the management of change. Therefore this unit not only examines our third scenario of growth, but consolidates our dual focus on enterprise and change.

To these ends we examine the nature of growth; analyse features of growth by using the Seven S Framework and TPF approaches; relate growth to specific expansion programmes; and conclude by citing some examples of the fine-tuning of this growth scenario.

B. Introduction

As we have seen in the last two units, some growth and development are important both to the steady state scenario and to the position of decline/recovery.

In this unit, we shall focus on more rapid growth as a scenario in its own right, rather than as a move or development of the two preceding scenarios (Units Four and Five).

There is a view that such growth should always be the dominant scenario, for without growth you suffer from decline relative to your competitors, who may still be growing. Whether or not we accept this viewpoint, there will be a need for some 'forced growth' whereby management almost manufactures the preconditions of the growth scenario. We will develop these ideas in the next few sections. In the interim, please tackle Activity ECM6.1. Then consult Box ECM6.1 for one 'solution' to the activity, and Box ECM6.2, which widens the debate about growth.

ACTIVITY ECM6.1

GROWTH AND MORE GROWTH

Activity code

- ✓ Self-development
- ☐ Teamwork
- ✓ Communications
- ☐ Numeracy/IT
- ✓ Decisions

Task

'There is an infatuation with business growth – almost for its own sake.' Discuss.

BOX ECM6.1

Growth and unused resources

Penrose believes that firms grow when there are unused resources in the business. These unused resources are generated as a result of change and the accumulation of experience and new knowledge. In fact, unused managerial resources are necessary for expansion, since if managers are completely absorbed in the problems of current production there can be no space for planning and taking on new developments. It is unlikely, therefore, that the textbook model of perfect competition would be conducive to growth. Managers would be unable to devote the necessary resources to R & D, for instance, since they would be concentrating on the current marketing and production problems.

Alongside the ability to grow there must also be a desire to grow. The status and rewards of managers are more positively related to size than they are to profitability. At the same time, a growing firm offers rapid promotion up the managerial ladder. Thus for internal labour markets to be effective the firm has to adapt to changing conditions and grow. This explains the different emphasis on growth in firms where shareholders and management are separated and those where they are the same people.

In markets which are expanding, growth is part of the competitive process, since to stand still is to fall behind. The fast-growing firm will tend to have a higher profitability, lower prices or better-quality products, or some combination of these. At the same time, expanding firms will attract and retain better managers and workers because of the increased opportunities and resources available.

Source:

1 Adapted from Penrose, E.T., *The Theory of the Growth of the Firm* (Blackwell Publishers, Oxford, 1966).

BOX ECM6.2

If we do not grow, do we decline?

Organizational growth can become a fetish, but there may be truth in the claim that if we do not grow and others do, we go into a relative decline.

There seem to be several approaches to looking at growth:

- **Planned evolution.** This takes a mathematical formula-type approach. Growth is based on percentage or proportion and linked to financial indicators such as dividend or returns, new investment or profitability, etc. Thus evolution becomes a target-based approach and the growth is forced.
- **Unplanned revolution.** Change or metamorphosis comes through some radical sudden change. It is not percentage x on the year before, but some sudden venture – usually unplanned if not accidental.
- **Some combination of revolution and evolution.** Elements of both planning and lack of planning seem to be involved in this approach.

The motives behind choosing to grow may be more positive than keeping pace with the competition. For example, growth could be motivated by:

- power;
- greater job security;
- risk and innovation;
- adventure and change;
- possible economies of scale;
- more profit or greater return;
- more products or a greater portfolio;
- beating the opposition or forming a monopoly;
- the perception that growth may mean greater stability in the long run, provided that change does not occur for its own sake.

A strategic business unit (SBU), as mentioned earlier, is a business which serves a distinct product/market segment, a well-defined set of customers, or a geographic area. It can be managed independently of other businesses and is defined by the products/services it provides, the customers it serves and the technology and functions it uses to provide the products/services. See figures ECM4.1 and ECM4.2 (Unit Four).

Most companies start as small SBUs which serve a local or regional market. The early years are characterized by few products/services, little capital and a weak competitive position. Efforts are concentrated on increasing sales and market share and developing a loyal customer base. Profits are reinvested and debt used to grow the enterprise as fast as possible. Product, price, promotion and distribution are tailored to customer needs.

As soon as possible, the product/service line is widened and the geographical area extended. At some point consideration is given to vertical integration (dealt with later in this unit), either backwards to the raw materials or forwards towards the consumer. This can be done by internal expansion, acquisitions or co-operation. The same can be said for gaining market share. Such developments usually continue until growth opportunities in the industry begin to diminish and then consideration has to be given to diversification in its various forms (see figure ECM6.1).

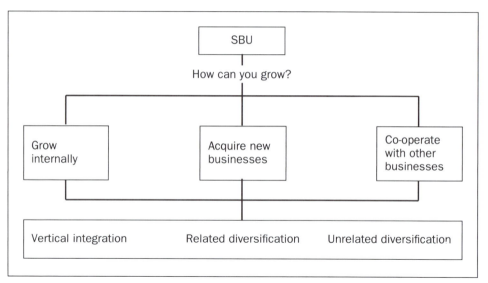

Figure ECM6.1 Various approaches to growing a business.

The business has to decide whether to continue in the same industry and:

- grow internally;
- acquire new businesses in related industries;
- co-operate with other enterprises; or
- acquire new businesses in unrelated industries.

Once the business has grown, there comes a time for taking stock of the situation. Should expansion continue and the business eventually go global, or is there a need for restructuring?

The growth of a business is the result of having sufficient financial resources, good products/services, expanding markets, favourable external environmental conditions, and skilled management with time available to take on the extra work involved. Decisions about expansion are based on the management's ability to assess these variables accurately. At the same time, size is important, since a small firm cannot compete effectively if it lacks production capacity or market strength. Nor can a firm compete if it is so large it is unmanageable with its current structure.

Managers believe a growing business is healthy and so by expanding their businesses that they are shown to be effective managers. Many managers like to leave behind them a business that is larger than it was when they started. Other managers believe growth ensures long-term survival, since if one product fails a large business will not suffer a major loss, whereas it may spell disaster for a small business.

If a business is strong and the environment is favourable then the firm will usually decide to grow. Growth or expansion means producing new products or services, entering new markets or developing new roles. According to Luffman et al.,[2] this can be carried out in three ways (see figure ECM6.2):

1 by internal expansion;
2 through acquisitions;
3 by co-operation.

	Internal expansion	Acquisitions	Co-operation
Products	Develop new products	Acquire firms	Joint ventures Minor interest
Markets	Develop new markets	Vertical integration Related diversification	Licences Franchises
Roles	Develop new roles		Subcontractors Selling agents
		Unrelated diversification	Networks

Figure ECM6.2 Various ways of growing a business through its products, markets and roles.

The growth or expansion of a business involves either or both of:

1 the addition of new products/services, new markets and/or new roles;
2 an increase in the effort employed by the business to increase efficiency, sales and profits. This could, for instance, involve finding new uses for products, gaining market share and/or increasing capacity.

Growth very often involves investment and an increase in risk. In fact, growth is not always good for a business, since inefficiencies may result in lower profits, and there may be monopoly problems or the development of fierce competition. On the other hand, growth is more likely in a volatile, highly competitive industry and may be necessary for survival. There is also the possibility that it could result in improved performance.

A business may choose to grow either internally, through acquisitions or through co-operation. **Internal expansion** means investment within the enterprise, whereas growth through **acquisitions** means investing outside the business, and **co-operation** could involve both internal and external investment.

C. Growth

In this section we describe a growth scenario in order to set the scene for the various methods of growth which we shall analyse later.

A possible scenario may include some of the following:

- Politically the government may be helpful with tax relief, reduced duties and assistance schemes.

- The economic scene may be encouraging new development.

- New markets may have developed through social changes.

- Your firm may have some technological edge over the competition and be beating the competition on an upward growth curve in demand.

The Seven S Framework

A growing business can be analysed using the Seven S Framework. The **strategy** is assumed to be successful or the organization would not be planning to expand. The methods which can be used for expansion have been outlined above. The success encourages more investment and risk taking.

The possibilities for changes in **structure** are described later, but any such changes must facilitate the strategy.

The expansion of any organization places great strains on the **systems** of an organization. The key factors are outlined in Unit Five.

Managing the growth of an organization is about managing change, and in order to do this you need to have a vision of the future and be able to communicate it to others. You also need to be able to perceive opportunities for change and be able to use political and other skills to manage change. Rowe et al.[3] identify four different decision **styles** of managers based on research studies. They provide a decision style inventory, which has been used with thousands of managers since 1977 (see figure ECM6.3).

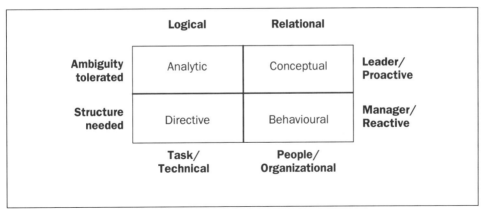

Figure ECM6.3 Decision style model.
Source: Adapted from Rowe, A.J., Mason, R.O., Dickel, K.E. and Snyder, N.H., *Strategic Management: a methodological approach* (Addison-Wesley, Reading, MA, 1990).

The **directive** style is associated with the need for power and the **behavioural** style with the need for affiliation. The **analytical** style needs achievement and the **conceptual** style needs recognition. Although decision makers may have a dominant style, they should try to use different styles according to the situation.

This model is based on the idea of four forces which influence the decision maker (see figure ECM6.4). This is a development of figure ECM3.6 above (Unit Three).

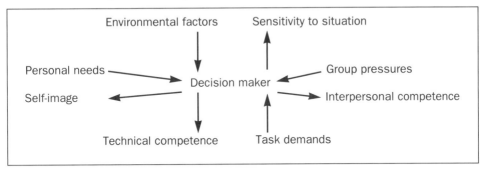

Figure ECM6.4 The Four Force Model for decision making.
Source: Rowe, A.J., Mason, R.O., Dickel, K.E. and Snyder, N.H., *Strategic Management: a methodological approach* (Addison-Wesley, Reading, MA, 1990).

See also Box ECM6.3 on the key competencies for change agents, which we believe are critical features in any drive for change.

BOX ECM6.3

Key competencies for change agents

Buchanan and Boddy identified fifteen key competencies for change agents:

Goals	Sensitivity to change
	Clarity in specifying goals
	Flexibility in responding to change
Roles	Team building ability
	Networking skills
	Tolerance of ambiguity
Communication	Communication skills
	Interpersonal skills
	Personal enthusiasm
	Motivating skills
Negotiation	Selling skills
	Negotiating skills
Managing	Political awareness
	Influencing skills
	Broad viewpoint

Source:
Adapted from Buchanan, D. and Boddy, D., *The Expertise of the Change Agent: public performance and backstage activity* (Prentice Hall, Englewood Cliffs, NJ, 1992).

The decision style required will vary with the situation and the role or task of the manager. Therefore managers need to assess themselves in order to make the best of any situation. At the same time, they should be able to assess one another's decision-making capabilities in order to take advantage of any situation.

Please tackle Activity ECM6.2.

Staff are a major factor in expansion. Current staff have to be motivated, trained and developed to grow with the organization. The staff of acquired organizations have to be shed or absorbed. New staff have to be planned for. All of this activity implies great stress on human resources management.

Skills are those activities which the organization does best, and are to be found in the value chain. New skills and competencies may need to be developed as the business grows.

The communication of **shared values** is important during a period of growth in order that the growing organization becomes a coherent whole.

Now please complete Activity ECM6.3.

ACTIVITY ECM6.2

DECISION-MAKING STYLE

Activity code

- ✓ Self-development
- ☐ Teamwork
- ☐ Communications
- ☐ Numeracy/IT
- ☐ Decisions

Task

Reflect on your own decision-making style using the information given so far. Classify your style, with an appropriate rationale.

ACTIVITY ECM6.3

VISION AND OBJECTIVES

Activity code

- ✓ Self-development
- ☐ Teamwork
- ✓ Communications
- ✓ Numeracy/IT
- ✓ Decisions

Tasks

1 Refer back to Activity ECM4.3 (Unit Four) and assess your own organization, then write a vision statement.
2 Now write some performance objectives for 'your' organization or college (see Unit Four).

D. Change and Enterprise Management

Growth involves continuous change. This must be managed carefully in order to accommodate the stresses and strains involved in the growth process. At the same time, managers need to be enterprising in order to take advantage of the opportunities and possibly to turn the threats into opportunities. Therefore, in order to grow successfully, managers must organize the business in such a way that they have the time and energy to devote to the growth process.

Many managers simply think in terms of obtaining the money to expand, but there is more to it than that. Expansion means retaining the synergy between the Seven Ss and giving oneself the time and space to concentrate on expansion.

The next two sections will outline the various ways of expanding both internally and externally. Growth involves leadership and vision – both inherent in the TPF analytical technique – and we will return to these key issues later.

Internal expansion

Internal expansion usually involves the business in trying to increase its sales and market share and so increase its profits significantly. This process can be easily understood by considering figure ECM6.5.

	Present products	New products
Present markets	Gain market share with current products 1	Add new products Risky 2
New markets	Add new markets Risky 3	Add new products and markets High risk 4

Figure ECM6.5 How growth can occur through developing products and markets.

In cell 1 of figure ECM6.5, the business tries to develop sales by encouraging demand and new uses for its present products and services in the markets it currently serves. Investment in marketing is needed and pricing and promotion can be useful. Gaining market share can be costly and may need to be associated with increased efficiency.

In cell 2, the business has to develop new products and services for the current markets. This can involve investment in R & D and the production processes.

In cell 3, the business tries to gain markets – both customers and geographical areas. Investment is required in marketing and distribution channels.

In cell 4, new products, services and markets all have to be developed, and this involves investment in R & D, production processes, marketing and distribution channels.

As soon as the business moves away from the present markets and products it takes risks, and failure rates can be high.

Internal growth by **penetration** implies growth by increasing market share and sales with the current products/services. The advantage of this is that managers are familiar with the products/services and markets. The disadvantage is that if the market is stable, and you try to expand, competitors may retaliate. Therefore, internal growth is usually best in an expanding market.

Internal growth involves moving into new geographic areas, modifying the product/service to provide new features by using differentiation creatively.

Internal **start-up** by getting a new business started and operating in an industry involves developing knowledge, resources, facilities and market reputation to compete effectively.

Internal start-up also involves overcoming entry barriers, investing in capacity, developing sources of supply, hiring and training employees, developing distribution channels and a customer base, etc. This is usually most attractive when:

- there is plenty of time;
- competitors are likely to be slow in retaliating;
- internal start-up has lower costs than an acquisition;
- the business has the necessary skills and technology to compete effectively;
- the new capacity will not affect the supply/demand balance of the industry;
- the industry has many small businesses, so it does not have to compete with larger more powerful ones.

You can also look at the functions your organization performs. In other words, how does it add value? In order to find this out you need to examine the value chain to discover new ways to add value to your products or services. This may involve vertical integration, new processes and new technology.

Now read Box ECM6.4 about the risk of launching a new business, then tackle Activity ECM6.4.

BOX ECM6.4

Launching a new business is risky

Companies often grow by launching new businesses into product markets where they have not previously competed. This approach complements the **product portfolio** concept, which argues that for a company to grow it must mix established and new businesses.

Biggadike studied a sample of mainly industrial goods businesses from the top 200 of the *Fortune* '500' and data from PIMS. He found that it takes an average of eight years for a new venture to reach profitability, and ten to twelve years before the ROI of new ventures equals that of mature businesses (17 per cent).

He advises the rapid building of market share, despite the adverse effect this might have on the financial performance in the early years. This means that large-scale entry is necessary for a company that wants to grow through the addition of a new venture.

In view of this research, managers should answer the following questions:

■ How much are you prepared to spend over the eight years expected to reach profitability?
■ Will it be cheaper or easier to acquire a business already making and selling or able to make and sell the proposed product?

Source:
Adapted from Biggadike, E.R., 'The risky business of diversification', *Harvard Business Review*, May/June (1979), pp. 105–11.

ACTIVITY ECM6.4

INTERNAL GROWTH?

Activity code
☑ Self-development
☐ Teamwork
☑ Communications
☐ Numeracy/IT
☑ Decisions

Task

1 Examine 'your' organization or college and decide whether it can expand internally. Explain your answer.
2 Outline an action plan for expanding internally.

External expansion

Acquisitions

The acquisition of an existing business is another means of gaining market share and entering new markets and industries. It has the advantage of making a significant increase in market share or of gaining a quick entry into the target market/industry; it overcomes entry barriers such as technology and suppliers; the business quickly becomes large enough to match competitors on efficiency and unit costs; it avoids costs of advertising and promotion to gain market share and brand recognition; and it gains adequate distribution quickly, whereas internal development may disturb the supply/demand balance in the industry.

Entry by acquisition is often considered more costly than internal development, since costs are not distributed in the same way. The replacement costs of the assets may be greater than buying the company, especially as the distribution networks, personnel and production capacity, etc., are all in place.

The acquisition of another business may not necessarily involve cash outlay, since shares or loan stock can be involved. However, increasing capital in this way will dilute existing shareholders' interests and may cause a resistance to development amongst them.

The business enters the new market with the benefit of the experience already developed by the acquired company, which is established in a market or industry. The firm is part-way along the experience curve and so derives efficiencies difficult to develop in the early years of internal development.

The biggest challenge is to integrate the acquisition successfully in order to justify the costs/premium involved in the purchase.

For unrelated diversification, a decision about acquiring a business is based largely on financial criteria. Has the business the financial resources to acquire the target? Is the acquisition needed to improve overall performance? Is the timing right in terms of management being able to devote enough time to the acquisition? The search is one for attractive financial returns in any industry.

The acquiring firm has to decide whether to buy a successful business at a high price or a struggling business at a low price. It depends on the situation, the managers concerned and the cost-of-entry test.

The **cost-of-entry test** implies that the expected profit stream from the acquired business will provide a good return on the total acquisition cost (cost of preparation plus cost of acquisition) and any new capital required to sustain or expand its operations.[4]

Suppose a business making a profit after tax of £200,000 on capital of £1,000,000 (20 per cent return on capital employed, or ROCE) is purchased for £2,000,000. This means that in order for the acquiring business to make the same ROCE of 20 per cent, it would have to make a profit after tax of £400,000. Such calculations demonstrate that future profits are reflected in the purchase prices and it is difficult for the acquiring business to make a sufficient return on its investment to justify the considerable outlay.

The expansion or growth of a business normally occurs by acquisitions, mergers, joint ventures or internal development. Mergers or acquisitions are often chosen as the routes to expansion, but 50 per cent or more are unsuccessful. This is usually because of the high premiums, the debt incurred to fund the purchase, and the failure to produce synergy. Let us now examine some of the reasons for these failures.

When you buy another business you are making an investment and the basic principles of capital investment decisions apply.[5] This means that you should only proceed if the purchase makes a net contribution to shareholders' wealth. Many managers find this is a difficult decision because:

- benefits and costs are difficult to define;
- tax, legal and accounting issues must be taken into account;
- few managers understand the purpose of mergers or acquisitions and who gains and loses by them.

In order to measure the worth of an investment, we need to consider the value of the current and future benefits arising from it. If at all possible, these benefits should be expressed in terms of cash flows. However, the value of cash flows in the future, measured by current standards, must be less than that of the same cash flows today. Therefore, the cash flows must be multiplied by a discount factor or rate of return (often known as the discount rate, hurdle rate or opportunity cost of capital).

An investment must make a **net** contribution to value; therefore the net present value (NPV) is found by subtracting the investment required from the present value (PV):

$$NPV = PV - \text{Investment}$$

In this assessment we must also take account of **risk**. Some investments are riskier than others. Therefore, you should use a discount rate which also reflects the riskiness of the investment. This discount rate is often known as the **opportunity cost** of capital, because it is the return foregone by your investment. You could instead, perhaps, invest in the stock market, if that is of equivalent risk. In that case your opportunity cost of capital would be equivalent to the average return you would get by investing in a portfolio of stocks in similar businesses.

There seem to be two main rules for investments:

1 The **net present value rule** – only make investments which have positive net present values;

2 The **rate of return rule** – only make investments which offer rates of return in excess of their opportunity costs of capital.

Let us take a very simple case and suppose you are the manager of firm A and you wish to buy firm B. Will there be any economic gain from the purchase? There will only be one if the firms are worth more together than apart.

$$
\begin{aligned}
\text{Gain} &= \text{Present value (A + B)} - \text{Present value A + Present value B} \\
\text{Gain} &= \text{PVAB} - (\text{PVA} + \text{PVB})
\end{aligned} \tag{1}
$$

However, there will also be a cost for the purchase, which will depend on how the purchase is financed. Let us suppose the purchase is made using cash:

$$
\text{Cost} = \text{Cash} - \text{PVB} \tag{2}
$$

The net present value (NPV) of A purchasing B is measured by the difference between the gain and the cost:

$$
\begin{aligned}
\text{NPV} &= \text{Gain} - \text{Cost} \\
&= \text{PVAB} - (\text{PVA} + \text{PVB}) - (\text{Cash} - \text{PVB})
\end{aligned} \tag{3}
$$

You should only go ahead with the purchase if the NPV is positive.

For example: firm A has a present value of £1,000,000 and firm B a present value of £200,000. The purchase of firm B would result in cost savings for the combined business of a present value of £150,000.

Therefore, using equation (1):

$$
\begin{aligned}
\text{PVAB} &= \text{Gain} + \text{PVA} + \text{PVB} \\
&= £150,000 + £1,000,000 + £200,000 \\
&= £1,350,000
\end{aligned}
$$

Now suppose B is bought to £250,000 cash and we use equation (2):

$$
\begin{aligned}
\text{Cost} &= \text{Cash} - \text{PVB} \\
&= £250,000 - £200,000 \\
&= £50,000
\end{aligned}
$$

This shows that the shareholders in B have gained £50,000, and their gain is your cost. They have gained £50,000 of the £150,000 purchase gain. In other words, your gain is only £100,000, not £150,000 as you expected earlier. This can be confirmed using equation (3):

$$
\begin{aligned}
\text{NPV} &= \text{Gain} - \text{Cost} \\
&= \text{PVAB} - (\text{PVA} + \text{PVB}) - (\text{Cash} - \text{PVB}) \\
&= £1,350,000 - (£1,000,000 + £200,000) - (£250,000 - £200,000) \\
&= £100,000
\end{aligned}
$$

Brealey and Myers[6] explore this approach in some detail.

If both A and B were public companies quoted on the Stock Exchange and investors had not anticipated the purchase of B by A, then the announcement of the purchase would cause the value of B's shares to rise by £50,000. This means B is now valued at £250,000 – a rise of 25 per cent. If investors shared the management's assessment of the purchase, then the market value of A's shares would increase by £100,000 or 10 per cent.

From this example it appears that sellers normally gain from a purchase, whereas buyers may not gain very much relative to the costs and effort required to make the purchase.

Therefore, it pays to observe what the investors think will be the gains or costs of the purchase. If the share price of the buyer does not change or falls, then investors either believe the benefits of the purchase are doubtful or the buyer is paying too much.

When you estimate the benefits of a purchase, do not discount the cash flows of the combined firm to give an estimate of PVAB. Instead, concentrate on the **changes in cash flow** as a result of the purchase. In other words, you must be able to demonstrate why the two businesses are worth more together than apart.

When you are selling a business, think about why you are selling it. For instance, if you think it is unprofitable and should be sold, then unless a buyer can run the business better than you can yourself, the price you receive will reflect the poor prospects of that business. No doubt these are already reflected in your share price.

Following on from this, some managers only buy into firms that are selling below book value. However, unless the buyer can somehow add value by giving that firm a competitive edge, then the buyer will lose money.

You must also think about the implications when firms bid against one another for a target firm. Will the target be worth more to you than to the other bidders? If the answer is no, then do not bid. Even if you were to win such a contest, you would have paid too much, and if you lost, you would have wasted time and money preparing for it.

Several reasons can be given for buying another business or corporation, such as economies of scale, economies of vertical or horizontal integration, unused tax shields, combined complementary resources, as a use for surplus funds, to improve operations, to improve cash flow or to exploit unused debt capacity.

There are also several reasons which do not always result in increasing shareholder value. For instance, diversification is easier and cheaper for the shareholder than the corporation, as indicated earlier.

Increasing **earnings per share (EPS)** is often given as a reason for a merger or acquisition. A high EPS may indicate that investors believe that the firm has good growth prospects or its earnings are low. A low EPS value means the opposite.

However, EPS values are dependent on what the firm means by earnings, since these are book or accounting figures and, as such, reflect accounting procedures, which are not standard. These include the treatment of depreciation, valuation of stock, the way the accounts of merged firms are combined, the way R & D is capitalized or charged for, or the way tax liabilities are reported. All of these have an impact on the reported earnings of a business and can seriously affect the EPS values.

It should also be noted that EPS ignores not only cash flow but also risk, both of which are important in assessing whether a business will increase shareholder value.

Following on from this, suppose your business has a high price/earnings ratio because investors believe your business will have rapid growth in future earnings. You could satisfy these expectations, for example, by capital investment, product improvement or increased operating efficiency. However, instead, you might decide to grow by buying companies. If you were to buy slow-growing firms with low price/earnings ratios, your EPS would increase in the short term, but in the long term growth would slow down and earnings drop (see figure ECM6.6).

Before company A merges with company B, 100p invested in company A produces 10p of earnings and rapid growth prospects. However, 100p invested in company B before the merger produces 5p of earnings but slower growth prospects. The growth is shown by the steepness of the graph lines. If the total market value is not altered by the merger then 100p invested in the merged company produces 7p of earnings but slower growth. Company B loses in earnings but gains faster growth.

In order to maintain growth, company A has to keep buying slow-growing companies with low price/earnings ratios. Eventually, growth will slow down and stop, earnings will fall and company A will fail. This is because company A has not grown, for instance, by capital investment, product improvement or increased efficiency.

An advantage of an acquisition or merger is that, other things being equal, the probability of financial distress should decrease. There will also be a net gain from an acquisition or merger if it will allow an increase in borrowing and increased value from the interest tax shields.

External growth or expansion involves the investment of capital in other businesses with a view to vertical integration, related diversification or unrelated diversification. In order to acquire an enterprise to satisfy one of these objectives, criteria need to be selected on which to base judgements. Does the acquisition make sense?

Rowe et al.[7] provide an example of an acquisition search in which they provide such criteria. Managers need to identify possible targets and determine the:

1 stand-alone capabilities of the target business;

2 synergistic effects when merged;

3 risks involved with the merger or takeover.

Under (1), each target should be ranked against criteria such as:

■ size

■ growth

■ brands

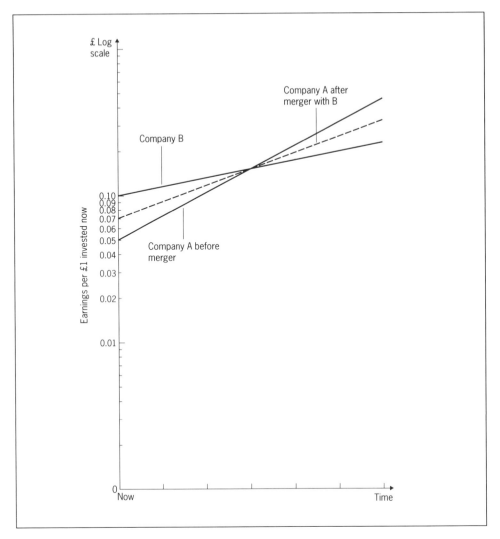

Figure ECM6.6 Effect of buying companies with low price/earnings ratios.
Source: Adapted from Brealey, R.A. and Myers, S.C., *Principles of Corporate Finance* (McGraw-Hill, Singapore, 1988).

- market share
- profitability
- asset utilization
- leverage
- efficiency of operations
- international network
- information and reporting systems
- proprietary technologies and patents
- availability of target, etc.

Under (2), the different types of synergies are examined:

- cost synergies
- price synergies
- other synergies.

Under (3), the risks involved in the merger or takeover of the target should be identified as:

- loss of key personnel
- loss of market share
- threat of competitor retaliation
- loss of image in the marketplace.

Vertical integration will be described later, but when it is considered as a possibility we must look for those firms which can be acquired without paying too high a price.

Related diversification (also described later) involves buying competitors with similar products or market segments. The intention is to buy either sales or production facilities in order to improve the long-term average cost curve and gain increased economies of scale. At the same time, you should also gain synergies from the combined markets, technologies and/or channels of distribution.

Please tackle Activity ECM6.5. Then please read Boxes ECM6.5 and ECM6.6 before you go any further.

ACTIVITY ECM6.5

PREREQUISITES OF DIVERSIFICATION

Activity code
- ✓ Self-development
- ✓ Teamwork
- ☐ Communications
- ☐ Numeracy/IT
- ✓ Decisions

Task

To consolidate the work so far on diversification, can you or your group derive certain prerequisites for successful diversification?
   NB Tackle this activity **before** reading Box ECM6.5 on diversification.

BOX ECM6.5

Diversification

The word 'diversification' often arises when considering the development of a business. Diversification changes the basic nature of the business in some way; for example, by acquiring new businesses in related or unrelated areas, or by investing in new ventures. There are the added complications of operating in new and unfamiliar areas, but the risk may be justified for those firms limited by strong competition, or with restricted markets, or which have uncertainties in their supply and distribution channels.

Porter studied the track record of thirty-three corporations with a reputation for good management between 1950 and 1986 and found that most of them had divested more acquisitions than they had kept.[1] Each corporation entered an average eighty new industries and twenty-seven new fields: 70 per cent were acquisitions, 22 per cent start-ups and 8 per cent joint ventures. On average the corporations divested more than 50 per cent of their acquisitions in new industries and 60 per cent of their acquisitions in new fields. Thus even these successful corporations have dissipated rather than created shareholder value – what a waste!

Porter believes there are certain premises which must be followed for successful diversification:

- **Competition occurs at the business unit level.** Diversified companies do not compete but their business units do. Successful corporations grow out of and nurture competitive business units.
- **Diversification inevitably adds costs and constraints to business.** Corporate overheads are obvious, but what about the effort spent explaining and complying with corporate systems, amongst other things?
- **Shareholders can easily diversify themselves** more cheaply than a corporation, which has usually to pay a premium for an acquisition. Thus a corporation cannot be successful unless it adds value to business units and to shareholders.

In order to decide whether a diversification will increase shareholder value, Porter applies three tests:

1 **The attractiveness test.** The industry chosen must produce consistently good returns on investment, have favourable competitive conditions, and have a market environment conducive to long-term profitability. Early growth does not mean long-term profit potential.

2 **The cost-of-entry test.** The cost of entry must not be so high as to erode profitability. Phillip Morris is reputed to have paid four times the book value for Seven-Up, and ultimately had to sell it because they could not make the investment pay.

3 **The better-off test.** The diversifying firm must bring some advantage to the business it buys or the new business must offer some extra competitive advantage to the firm. There should be an opportunity to create a sustainable competitive advantage where none existed before, and so increase profitability and shareholder value. Diversifying corporate risk does not satisfy the better-off test, since shareholders can normally diversify more cheaply themselves.

Diversifications must satisfy all three tests in order for them to build shareholder value over the long term.

Source:

1 Adapted from Porter, M.E., 'From competitive advantage to corporate strategy', *Harvard Business Review*, 45 (1987), pp. 46–9.

BOX ECM6.6

Creating shareholder value

Porter outlines three options for creating shareholder value: restructuring, transferring skills, and sharing activities.[1]

Restructuring

This seeks out undeveloped, sick or threatened businesses or industries on the threshold of significant change.

Restructuring passes the three tests of successful diversification. Cost of entry is met by the types of company bought; the better-off test is clearly met; and businesses are only bought if the industry is structurally attractive.

Transferring skills

The value chain is useful for identifying an activity which creates synergy. This is the ability to transfer skills or expertise among similar value chains. Even though the units operate separately, the similarities in the value chains allow sharing of knowledge and skills.

Three conditions must be satisfied in order for the transference of skill to lead to competitive advantage:

1 The business activities must be so similar that sharing expertise is meaningful.
2 The transfer of skills must involve activities which are important for competitive advantage.
3 The skills transferred must provide a significant competitive advantage for the receiving business.

The idea is to satisfy two of the diversification tests by offsetting the acquisition premium and/or lower the cost of overcoming entry barriers. The attractiveness test must still be strictly adhered to in order to ensure success.

The transfer of skills should be ongoing; if it happens once only, then the acquired business should be sold on.

Sharing activities

Another source of synergy which can be defined by the value chain is the sharing of activities between business units, such as the sharing of distribution channels or research and development. This sharing leads to competitive advantage by lowering costs or enhancing differentiation.

Sharing activities, however, also involves the costs of managing them and the compromises needed to enable the activities to be shared.

For this approach to be successful the corporation must have:

- a strong sense of corporate identity;
- a clear mission statement that emphasizes the integration of business units;
- an incentive system that rewards more than just business unit results;
- cross-unit task forces;
- other methods of integrating.

Shared activities clearly meet two of the tests for creating shareholder value: the better-off test, because the units gain tangible advantages from one another, and the cost-of-entry test, by reducing the barriers to entry. The attractiveness test must still be strictly adhered to in order to be sure of success.

The secret of the success of Porter's research is that corporations can employ a restructuring policy at the same time as they transfer skills and/or share activities. This means the activities are not mutually exclusive, but reinforce one another.

Porter found that successful corporations had a very low percentage of unrelated acquisitions. 'Unrelated' means that there is little or no opportunity to transfer skills or share key activities. This means that successful corporations diversify into areas which are related and synergy develops by transferring skills and sharing activities.

Successful corporations also have good records for start-ups and joint ventures. This is probably because of the high costs of integration. The Japanese normally diversify by start-up or joint venture.

It would seem that the correct industry structure and the right implementation policies are prerequisites for all of the three options to work.

Source:
1 Adapted from Porter, M.E., 'From competitive advantage to corporate strategy', *Harvard Business Review*, 45 (1987), pp. 46–9.

Vertical integration

The objective of vertical integration, according to Thompson and Strickland,[8] is to strengthen an organization's competitive position. Vertical integration must produce cost savings or a competitive advantage to justify the extra investment. Integration can be backwards, towards the source of raw materials, or forwards, towards the customer. Backward integration only generates cost savings when the production volume is big enough to capture the same economies of scale or production efficiency as competitors, or better.

The value chain concept and the opportunity to differentiate products and services are important considerations.

In terms of rules, growth or expansion can mean adding a distribution channel or making rather than buying components. Consideration of the value chain of the business may cause managers to consider the possibilities of vertical integration. This involves the business in expanding the functions performed. For example, a business buys in some input, adds value by transforming it into output, and sells it on to a customer of some kind. This process occurs at different stages in the value chain for each business. The decision has to be taken whether the business should perform more of the value chain or not. Figure ECM6.7 shows how value is added in the value chain.

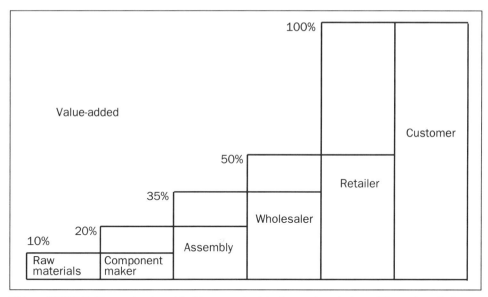

Figure ECM6.7 How value is added to a product in the major stages of the value chain.

Vertical integration allows ownership and control of the inputs to the production processes and distribution channels of a business. The objective is to extend the competitive scope of the business within the same industry. Vertical integration can enable cost centres to be converted to profit centres; develop economies of scale; enter new product or market segments; and improve the reliability of supply. Investment in vertical integration is only useful if it improves the competitive position or saves costs for the business.

Vertical integration is assumed to offer cost savings and better control over supplies, but each situation is different and must be judged on its merits. For example, Laura Ashley tried to continue being a vertically integrated company when it went international, but had problems with its cost base and distribution channels.

Backward integration will save costs when the volumes are large enough to capture the same economies of scale as the suppliers have and when the efficiency of the suppliers can be equalled or exceeded. The best cost advantage occurs when the suppliers have large profit margins, or the material/product is a major cost component of the final product, or the technology and skills are easy to develop. If a business can improve quality and service by backward integration, then a differentiation-based competitive advantage may be produced.

Backward integration reduces a business's dependence on suppliers for crucial materials, parts or services, and can also reduce its vulnerability to powerful suppliers that are able to raise prices when they wish.

Forward integration can produce similar savings. For instance, stock problems and underutilization of capacity are often a sign of poor sales or distribution problems. Forward integration can be better in some cases than selling through dealers and wholesalers.

A manufacturer that integrates forwards could use franchises or establish retail outlets. A raw materials producer that integrates forwards into manufacturing could develop greater product differentiation. Raw materials compete largely on price and are often commodity-like in that they have essentially the same technical specifications irrespective of who produces them. Competition tends to be fierce, with shifting supply and demand causing volatile profits. Thus the closer a product can be taken to the consumer the easier it is for a commodity-like supplier to differentiate products using design features, service, packaging, etc., and so gain additional profit margins.

Please tackle Activity ECM6.6 before reading Box ECM6.7.

ACTIVITY ECM6.6

VERTICAL INTEGRATION: POSSIBLE PROBLEMS

Activity code
- ✓ Self-development
- ☐ Teamwork
- ✓ Communications
- ☐ Numeracy/IT
- ✓ Decisions

Task

Outline possible problems with vertical integration.

BOX ECM6.7

Vertical integration: problems

Several problems are associated with vertical integration:

■ It causes the business to increase its investment in the industry, money which might be better spent developing products or markets.

- Risks are extended across a larger part of the value chain.
- The high capital investment can encourage a business to protect its investment in technology and facilities rather than replace them as they become obsolete. Fully integrated businesses are more vulnerable to new technologies and products than partially or non-integrated ones.
- There can be difficulties in balancing production capacities at various points in the value chain, since efficiency in each stage normally varies. Overproduction needs to be sold or stored and underproduction needs to be bought in. Any by-products also have to be sold or disposed of.

Thus vertical integration is unlikely to be attractive unless it:
- meets the long-term objectives of the business;
- creates a competitive advantage and so strengthens the business's competitive position in the industry.

Disintegration can also occur when a business subcontracts manufacturing, marketing, distribution and even money collection. This approach can reduce capital investment and add flexibility but can make a business vulnerable to subcontractors.

Related diversification

Related diversification[9] involves managers in identifying those new industries which have a good strategic fit with one or more of the corporation's current businesses. This means looking at the value chains of the targets and comparing them to the value chains of the businesses already in the corporation's portfolio.

For example, the better-off test can be satisfied through sharing R & D, joint production and assembly, marketing and distribution, customers, after-sales service and management – that is, where there is a fit between the two businesses in terms of marketing, production and/or management.

The next stage is to identify where the development of competitive advantage is possible through cost cutting or skill transfer. Much depends on the competitive advantage of the **strategic fit** benefits; how much it will cost to gain them; and how difficult it will be to merge and co-ordinate the two businesses. The bigger the competitive advantage of related diversification, the more it satisfies the better-off test.

Strategic fit can occur anywhere in the value chain and represents opportunities for cost saving, technology and skill transfer or other benefits of activity sharing.

Related diversification allows a business to keep a similarity in its activities, gain competitive advantage of skills transfer, lower costs and spread risks over a broader base. The business exploits what it does best and transfers its skills to other businesses.

Lower costs occur through managing two or more businesses under one management and from similar savings in the value chains. According to Thompson and Strickland,[10] strategic fit relationships fall into three broad categories:

1 **Market-related fit** occurs when the value chains of two or more businesses overlap so that the products are used by the same customers; distributed through the common dealers or retailers; marketed and promoted in similar ways.

    Several cost-saving opportunities can be envisaged: using a single sales force rather than one for each firm; advertising related products in the same adverts and brochures; using the same brand names; co-ordinating distribution and delivery; combining after-sales service and repairs; co-ordinating order processing and billing; using common promotion methods. All of these can reduce marketing, selling and distribution costs.

    There are also opportunities for the transfer of selling, promotion, advertising and product-differentiating skills from one business to the other.

2 **Operating fit** occurs when the value chains overlap so that there is a potential for cost sharing or skills transfer in procurement, R & D, technology, production, assembly or the performance of administrative support functions. Cost saving can result from economies of scale (combining activities into larger-scale operations) or economies of scope (doing things together rather than separately).

3 **Management fit** occurs when the businesses have similar types of management process, so that management skills can be easily transferred between the businesses. These transfers can occur anywhere in the value chain.

It is easy to recognize the benefits of strategic fit and diversify into such industries, but much harder actually to realize the benefits by merging the businesses into a single co-ordinated working unit. Merged functions and co-ordination often involve reorganization costs. You also need to ask the question: 'Is centralized control better than business unit autonomy?' Skills transfer is important for creating a competitive advantage. How can these changes be made without demotivating or even dismissing some of the workforce?

Related diversification is a strategic approach to creating shareholder value, because it is based on exploiting the links between the value chains of different businesses to lower costs, transfer skills and technology, and make other strategic fits. The objective is to gain a competitive advantage that is beyond what business subsidiaries are able to achieve on their own.

Unrelated diversification
Unrelated diversification[11] involves buying businesses which the management believe will provide a good profit opportunity. Managers try to meet the industry attractiveness and cost-of-entry tests, but the better-off test is secondary. Target businesses are identified using criteria such as the following:

- Does the business meet corporate targets for profits and ROI?
- Does the business require additional capital?
- Is the business in an industry with growth potential?
- Will the business contribute significantly to the bottom line?
- Is there any potential for conflict in terms of unions or government legislation?
- Is the industry vulnerable to recession, inflation, high interest rates or shifts in government policy?

Three types of business are particularly attractive for takeover:

1 businesses with **undervalued assets**, so that the assets can be split up and sold for more than they cost;

2 businesses in **financial distress**, if they can be bought at bargain prices and turned round with a capital injection and management skill – they can then either be kept as a long-term investment or sold on at a profit;

3 businesses which have **good growth prospects** but are starved of capital.

The advantages of unrelated diversification are that business risk is reduced by investing in a variety of industries and by offsetting up-and-down trade cycles. Capital can be invested in whichever industries offer the best profit prospects. Profitability is more stable, since hard times in one industry may be partly offset by good times in another. Shareholder wealth can be increased if management is good at spotting opportunities for profit.

The disadvantages are that top managers have to be able to make sound decisions in widely different industries and competitive environments. The performance of a conglomerate tends to be no better than the performance of the businesses involved, without some kind of strategic fit and added competitive advantage. The claim of greater stability over business cycles is rarely borne out in practice, since all businesses are affected during major economic cycles.

Unrelated diversification is a finance-driven approach to creating shareholder value, so managers must have superior skills at managing a portfolio of businesses. They must be able to:

- choose new businesses that produce consistently good ROI (industry attractiveness test);
- negotiate good acquisition prices (cost-of-entry test);
- sell on businesses at top prices;
- be skilled at transferring corporate resources from poor performers to good performers;
- manage the businesses so that they perform better (better-off test).

If managers can increase shareholder value at a greater rate than the shareholders can do themselves, then unrelated diversification is justified.

Now read Box ECM6.8 for a view of the global market, and tackle Activity ECM6.7.

BOX ECM6.8

Going global

Recent developments in information technology, TV and transportation have resulted in a customer-driven world economy. For instance, to what extent do you think that the changes in Eastern Europe and Russia over the last ten years have been the result of people in those countries learning about the lifestyle of the western world through the media? As the economies of the Eastern Bloc change, demand will rise for all types of products and services. This is also happening in the Third World countries, and so a customer-driven global economy is developing. The global corporation is emerging, and it will operate as if the world were a single market with headquarters, production and distribution facilities throughout the world. It is not centred on a single country, since national boundaries are meaningless to a global economy. Global corporations have a worldwide strategy rather than a strategy for each country.

On the other hand, understanding the cultures of different countries will be a basic requirement for the global manager. Body language, time concepts, greetings, spatial patterns and other symbols need to be appreciated. In order for trade to develop, the differences between cultures must be recognized and accommodated in designs and specifications for products and services.

For each country, its economic stability, market size, GNP, literacy and technology in terms of communications, transport and energy resources are critical for developing business. Also important for assessing foreign countries are the political and legal structures. These include government attitudes to public and private ownership, consumers and foreign trade (quotas, embargoes, duties, exchange controls, customs and entry procedures).

There are two major challenges for the global corporation. One is to provide product and service quality and so satisfy customer needs, and the other is to remain competitive. To improve quality and remain competitive is the major challenge of any manager, and this has led to **benchmarking**. This is the continuous process of measuring products, practices and services against those of competitors and leaders in other industries. It is the value chain again – try measuring your distribution system against the best in any industry. In what ways can you improve your distribution system?

See also Anderson, A.H., Dobson, T. and Patterson, J., *Effective International Marketing* (Blackwell Publishers, Oxford, forthcoming).

ACTIVITY ECM6.7

ACQUISITION

Activity code
- ✓ Self-development
- ☐ Teamwork
- ✓ Communications
- ✓ Numeracy/IT
- ✓ Decisions

Tasks

1 Examine 'your' organization or college and decide whether it can expand by acquisition. Explain your answer.
2 Outline an action plan for expanding by acquisition.

Co-operation

Internal growth and the acquisition of businesses are at either end of a continuum for the expansion of a business. In between are other ways of developing new products, markets and functions, which involve co-operation between businesses. For example, one business may have an idea for a product and be able to produce it. However, it may not have the required marketing skills, so it may look for another business which has those skills to co-operate with it in finding and selling the product to customers.

A **joint venture** is jointly owned by two or more businesses and produces a product or service important to the owners. Shares in a joint venture may not be equal but will reflect the finance, technology or other inputs of the owners.

Joint ventures are useful for gaining access to distribution channels, supplies and technology. When resources are scarce, there is a high risk, technology changes quickly or large capital investment is required, joint ventures are often the best way for a small enterprise to gain market share and expand globally. They may also be a political necessity; for example, as a condition for entering a new market in a foreign country or, perhaps, when a local partner is necessary to overcome language or cultural barriers.

Strategic alliances occur when two firms combine resources beyond the limits of a joint venture. Trust is a major requirement for a strategic alliance.

According to Drucker,[12] joint ventures are good when a project is risky or uneconomical to undertake alone, or when pooling resources and skills produces a business with more of the skills to be a good competitor (that is, one partner brings skills and resources which are important to the success of the project and which the other does not have). Sometimes the only way to overcome import quotas, tariff barriers, national and cultural barriers is by a joint venture with a foreign enterprise. Domestic partners provide outside businesses with the benefits of local knowledge, management and distribution channels. Controls, procurement, quality and standards can cause problems for managers of the outsider.

Temporary collaborative ventures are often used for large projects such as R & D or civil engineering.

Selling agents can often be used to sell products. They enable a sales network to be established quickly and cheaply. However, the commitment and quality of the sales staff are not under the control of the business. Selling agents are useful in the early stages of the development of a market when local knowledge is important.

Licensing agreements are often used in order to penetrate markets quickly with products protected by patents. Some profit may be lost but investment capital is saved, and may be used in other ways.

Under such arrangements, one business agrees to allow another to make and/or sell the licensor's product and use the brand name. In return, the licensee pays the licensor a commission or royalty. The licensor can become involved in international trade with little financial risk. The licensee gains products and technology otherwise unobtainable. The payment is low (often about five per cent of sales). Licensing agreements usually last about ten years, and then the licensee may continue to market the product without paying the licensor. Licensing agreements also give away trade secrets for 5 per cent of the sales. Are they worth it?

Franchising is an agreement to permit another business to perform part of the business process for a fee or share of the profits. Training and other facilities are often offered. The franchiser provides the distinctive elements for the business – name, signs, facilities, designs, materials, standard products, etc. A franchise offers an established product or service, advertises a brand image, and should lower the risk of failure. On the other hand, it limits freedom and the ways of doing business.

Please read Box ECM6.9.

BOX ECM6.9

Co-operation

Joint development has become increasingly popular since the 1970s because businesses cannot always cope with the complex environment using internal resources alone. They need to obtain materials, skills, knowhow, finance and access to markets, and they realize these can be obtained just as easily through co-operation as through ownership.

There are different forms of co-operation, which are influenced by the extent to which:

- assets need to be managed jointly;
- it is possible to separate the assets involved between the partners involved;
- there is the risk of one of the partners involved appropriating the assets for themselves.

Formal integration
Acquisitions and mergers are likely to occur when:

- assets need joint management;
- assets cannot be separated easily from either enterprise involved;
- there is a risk of asset appropriation.

Formalized ownership/relationships
Consortia and joint ventures occur when:

- assets need to be jointly managed;
- assets/skills can be separated;
- there is low risk of assets being appropriated.

Contractual relationships
Subcontracting, licences and franchises are likely when:

- asset management can be isolated;
- assets/skills can be separated;
- there is a risk of assets being appropriated.

Loose (market) relationships
Networks and opportunistic alliances are likely when:

- assets do not need joint management;
- assets cannot be separated;
- there is high risk of assets being appropriated.

Networks are arrangements where two or more businesses work in collaboration without formal relationships, through a mechanism of mutual advantage and trust.

Opportunistic alliances are focused on particular ventures and projects which are more market-related than contractual relationships.

Source:
Adapted from Johnson, G. and Scholes, K., *Exploring Corporate Strategy: text and cases* (Prentice Hall, Hemel Hempstead, 1993).

Snow et al.[13] describe the **network organization** as a flexible relationship between manufacturers, buyers, suppliers and customers, which can be permanent or temporary. The members of the network can be changed to meet changing competitive conditions. Each member in a network concentrates on the activities it performs best. It is like putting together a value chain of the best performers of each activity in the industry. The members are held together by contracts and the pursuit of common goals.

Tully[14] has called this a **modular corporation** or hub surrounded by the best suppliers in the world. The hub is the centre of the activity, such as R & D, and the network consists of the outside specialists who make and assemble parts, handle distribution and perform collection and accounting services.[15]

A temporary network of independent businesses, which are linked by information technology and which can come together quickly to exploit fast-changing opportunities, has been called a **virtual corporation** by Byrne et al.[16]

E. Fine-tuning

This last section touches upon some examples of ways in which we can further refine our approach to growth.

Portfolio management

The management of the portfolio may have particular relevance to a diversified business. To Porter, portfolio management is not seen as creating or enhancing shareholder value, as portfolios are not sources of competitive advantage *per se*.[17] The approach of portfolio management may help in developing the organization, though, and we develop this at great length in another volume of this series.[18] Suffice it to say that the whole portfolio approach is based on the idea that each business unit generates or requires cash according to its position in the industry life cycle. For example, we can have a nine-cell matrix based on two dimensions: long-term industry attractiveness and the competitive position of the business.[19] A more sophisticated, fifteen-cell matrix, based on five stages of industry evolution and three levels of competitive position, has also been developed, and it helps to identify businesses which are very attractive or about to enter into decline.[20] Growth in these matrices may be linked to elements of risk taking, exploiting R & D initiatives in the early stages of the portfolio, and stricter cost controls when the business is in decline.

The Seven S Framework

Strategy

The strategy is obviously working and will encourage more investment and risk taking. Nevertheless, beware of turbulence in the environment. Costs and cash flow can easily get out of control.

Structure

As we have seen, the structure needs to reinforce the strategy. Simplicity seems to be the message, according to Drucker[21] and to Peters and Waterman, who recommend 'simple form, lean staff'.[22]

The one theme that we wish to pursue briefly here is that of **decentralization** and possible links to adaptability, enterprise and long-term growth.

The advantages of decentralization are believed to be: the release of pressure on top managers; better decisions, because they are made closer to the action; better training, morale and initiative at lower levels; faster decisions and more flexibility in changing environments.

We must be conscious of treating decentralization as a positive feature and centralization as indicative of a slow, bureaucratic organization. Decentralization without co-ordination and leadership is unacceptable and self-defeating.

The critical thing about the decentralized structure is that responsibility is pushed down through the organization. Thus responsibility centres develop for covering expenses, revenues, profits and investments in some cases. This can only spread the awareness of enterprise and the need to adapt and adopt right through the organization.

Systems

To monitor changes in both the external and internal environments and to be able to spot opportunities, we must have developed management and marketing information systems. One example of an intelligence system that is critical to our growth scenario is that of environmental scanning. The importance of environmental analysis can be seen in, say, competitive analysis. Please see Activity ECM6.8.

ACTIVITY ECM6.8

SYSTEMS: SCANNING THE COMPETITION

Activity code

☑ Self-development
☑ Teamwork
☑ Communications
☑ Numeracy/IT
☑ Decisions

Task

You (and/or your group) have been asked to determine what areas need to be built into a new system for scanning the competitive environment. This should include both quantitative and qualitative features for the new system. Use the chart below.

		Competitors			
Feature	Your business	A	B	C	D etc.
For instance:					
Market share by product:					
X					
Y					
Z					
etc.					

Style

Style is an aspect of overall leadership. Rather than go for one particular style to sustain growth, we should broaden the debate by talking about leadership and the TPF technique (covered below).

Staff

People are the organization. It is the commitment and expertise of the staff that differentiate one organization from another – particularly in the eyes of the buyer or customer of the products/services. It is the staff who provide the interface with the customer, not some obscure, remote concept of 'an organization'. Motivated staff, well rewarded intrinsically and extrinsically, can be a crucial factor in going for and sustaining growth.

Please complete Activity ECM6.9.

ACTIVITY ECM6.9

MOTIVATION AND SHARED ENTERPRISE

Activity code

- ☑ Self-development
- ☑ Teamwork
- ☑ Communications
- ☑ Numeracy/IT
- ☑ Decisions

In the preface we argued that entrepreneurship was linked to some form of ownership or real stake in the business. If this is the case, and we believe it is, then the entrepreneurial climate will perish as soon as we move away from the owners or from several key entrepreneurs in the business. One way forward is to devise an **employee share ownership plan (ESOP)**.

Task

Through individual or group effort:
1 Identify the objectives of such a plan.
2 Note the advantages and disadvantages of ESOPs to the major stakeholders.
3 Outline the mechanics of such a scheme.

The idea of 'empowerment' to meet the needs of a lean machine has already been covered in ECM Unit One. Rather than go down this route, the current view of competent, skilled staff giving some competitive advantage is relevant to our growth scenario.

This view is developed at length in our self-developmental text.[23] We have deliberately not gone down the route of the intrapreneur.

Please tackle Activity ECM6.10.

ACTIVITY ECM6.10

COMPETENCE, ENTERPRISE AND CHANGE

Activity code
- ✓ Self-development
- ✓ Teamwork
- ✓ Communications
- ✓ Numeracy/IT
- ✓ Decisions

The right skill mix, however so defined, which meets organizational and individual need, can only be a positive component of an enterprising organization. As such, as we have seen, it is one of the Seven Ss. UK organizations are moving away from talking about skill and more towards ideas of competence and competencies.

Task
Outline the competencies required for management to deal with enterprise and change.

This should be a major individual project or a team effort.

Skills
As a business grows, there is a tendency to lose sight of the skills/activities in the value chain which a business is good at and which give it its competitive edge.

Shared values
All through this book we have declined to say that the managerial value system needs to be accepted by the whole of the staff. Our aim is neither brainwashing nor attitudinal structuring. However, a customer orientation or a marketing approach to the business, epitomized by a view of quality from the perspective of the user, is one example of a legitimate shared value system.

Please refer to Box ECM6.10.

BOX ECM6.10

Quality

Quality is part of a climate of enterprise, as enterprise means exploiting marketing opportunity in line with both customer need and organizational strength.

Quality means meeting the customers' expectations of desired benefits. In theory, total quality would mean zero defects, but of course customer expectation and perception will differ, so we will not be able to please all of the people all of the time. So there is a positive aspect to quality in aspiring to meet customer needs.

Within the organization, the costs of not meeting quality standards or of error can be seen in the lack of repeat orders, losing customers, the costs of repair and servicing, legal cases, dissatisfied customers, and dissatisfied employees – no one wants to be identified with peddling garbage.

Initially, quality control with error detection during and after the event prevailed in some organizations. Now we have **quality assurance** and/or total quality management pervading organizations, and these are more problem-centred from the outset. The common denominator seems to be a striving towards zero defects linked to customer satisfaction. Quality standards and requirements are met, the idea permeates the work performance of all employees and managers, and it becomes not only a process but an attitude of mind – indeed, a philosophy linked to enterprise.

The TPF Perspective

An organization needs a leadership vision which permeates the whole body politic. It also needs key performance objectives derived from this vision, including corporate, divisional, departmental and individual key result areas.

Management that is going for growth, adapting to change and seeking opportunity needs not only clear policies and strategies, but a sound knowledge of the task and of the people who achieve that task. A functional, co-ordinative mechanism and an awareness of other disciplines of management can cement this view of leadership for the sake of the organization and of its people. This TPF Perspective, in the context of policy, vision and core objectives, goes a long way towards explaining the enterprise and change orientations of management in all of our three scenarios, including the growth situation. We develop this concept further in *Effective General Management*, which leads on from this text together with *Effective Business Policy*, in the 'enterprise' cluster of texts in this series.[24]

Perhaps, above all, though, enterprise and change management require **vision**. We have attempted to cultivate this insight over the last six units. Change and enterprise must be fused in order for both concepts to be understood and developed in the organization. This has been our vision in this book, and we hope that we have conveyed it convincingly.

Notes

1 Cited by Pascarella, P., 'The toughest turnaround of all', *Industry Week*, 2 April (1994).

2 Luffman, G., Sanderson, S., Lea, E. and Kenny, B., *Business Policy: an analytical introduction* (Blackwell Publishers, Oxford, 1987).

3 Rowe, A.J., Mason, R.O., Dickel, K.E. and Snyder, N.H., *Strategic Management: a methodological approach* (Addison-Wesley, Reading, MA, 1990).

4 See Porter, M.E., 'From competitive advantage to corporate strategy', *Harvard Business Review*, 45 (1987), pp. 46–9.

5 Brealey, R.A. and Myers, S.C., *Principles of Corporate Finance* (McGraw-Hill, Singapore, 1988).

6 Ibid.

7 Rowe et al., *Strategic Management*.

8 Thompson, A.A. and Strickland, A.J., *Strategic Management: concepts and cases* (Irwin, Holmewood, IL, 1992).

9 This section is based on Thompson and Strickland, *Strategic Management*.

10 Ibid.

11 This section is based on Thompson and Strickland, *Strategic Management*.

12 Drucker, P.F., *Management: tasks, responsibilities, practices* (Harper and Rowe, New York, 1974).

13 Snow, C.C., Miles, R.E. and Coleman, H.J., 'Managing 21st century network organisations', *Organisational Dynamics*, Winter (1992), pp. 5–19. See also Kilman, R.H., 'A networked company that embraces the world', *Information Strategy: The Executive Journal*, Spring (1990), pp. 23–6.

14 Tully, S., 'The modular corporation', *Fortune*, 8 February (1993), pp. 106–15.

15 See also Economist, 'Why networks may fail', *The Economist*, 10 October (1992), and Bush, J.B. and Frohman, A.L., 'Communication in a network organisation', *Organisation Dynamics*, Autumn (1991), pp. 23–36.

16 Byrne, J., Brandt, R. and Port, O., 'The virtual corporation', *Business Week*, 8 February (1993), pp. 98–102.

17 Porter, M.E., *Competitive Strategy: techniques for analyzing industries and competitors* (Free Press, New York, 1980).

18 Anderson, A.H. and Barker, D., *Effective Business Policy* (Blackwell Publishers, Oxford, 1994).

19 Allen, M.G., 'Diagramming GE's planning for what's WATT', in *Corporate Planning: techniques and applications*, eds R.J. Allio and M.W. Pennington (Amacom, New York, 1979).

20 Hofer, C.W. and Schendel, D., *Strategy Formulation: analytical concepts* (West Publishing Co., St Paul, MN, 1978).

21 Drucker, *Management*.

22 Peters, T.J. and Waterman, R.H., *In Search of Excellence* (Harper and Rowe, New York, 1982).

23 Anderson, A.H., Barker, D. and Critten, P., *Effective Self-Development* (Blackwell Publishers, Oxford, 1996).

24 Anderson, A.H., *Effective General Management* (Blackwell Publishers, Oxford, forthcoming), and Anderson and Barker, *Effective Business Policy*.

Conclusions

Instead of summarizing the whole book here, we shall highlight below some of the keynotes of the text. We believe that entrepreneurship is difficult to replicate in medium to large organizations, so a spirit of enterprise is suggested as an alternative, but related, concept.

The core idea is that managing change and managing enterprise are linked activities in the development of an organization. In order to adapt to change and adopt new ideas, organizations must be able to change, and a planned approach was put forward.

The external environments provide the opportunity for both change and enterprise, whereas the internal organizational environments are the motors of change and of enterprise. One of the core themes was the linking of externally oriented policies to internal organizational capacity. Enterprise from within the organization was seen as the motor to move things along.

Change and enterprise are not standardized formulae but are dynamic. We have tried to replicate this dynamism by examining three different scenarios which can face organizations: steady state, decline/recovery, and growth.

We have also attempted to move beyond these three scenarios to improve the health of the organization, enhance its enterprise capability and improve its capacity for change. The methods used include strategic insights, the Seven S Framework and the TPF Perspective.

In particular, the role of the 'staff' part of the Seven Ss was emphasized in this exposition. For managers, leadership and vision were seen as the key determinants of an enterprising culture, which meets the changing demands of both the internal and (especially) the external environments.

We have argued that a 'management revolution' occurs which separates the entrepreneurs/owners from the managers during the growth of the firm. This revolution is consolidated as the organization grows. In order for the organization to sustain itself during this growth phase, enterprise is required, unless, of course, some ownership is shared.

Managers need to develop their enterprise skills, especially as internal and external turbulence increase. By the end of the book, this vision of enterprise was required to pervade the whole organization. This implies that management *per se* is giving way to more inspired leadership.

In the next book of this 'enterprise' cluster in the series, *Effective Business Policy*,[1] we find even more structure within the organization and the danger of ossification occurring. Specialist planners and advisers flourish in the next phase of growth, while the management tends to become fatter and more removed from its customers. The concepts of change, enterprise, vision and leadership are just as important, although the scenarios may be more complex.

There may well be a move towards the marketing organization, with its belief in quality and the view that the business exists primarily to meet the needs of the customer. At the same time, the other stakeholders must not be neglected. Indeed, the other three clusters of books in the series – marketing, finance and people – support and cement these perspectives.

Note

1   Anderson, A.H. and Barker, D., *Effective Business Policy* (Blackwell Publishers, Oxford, 1994).

Index

209